GW00359650

Cuan Mhuire
A Haven of Hope

The life and work of Sister Consilio

Nora McNamara

HSI
PUBLICATIONS
3 Quinlan Street, Limerick, Rep. of Ireland
Phone: 061-317822 Fax: 061-317877 Email: hsi@iol.ie

First published in Rep. of Ireland in 2000 by HSI Publications
3 Quinlan Street, Limerick, Rep. of Ireland.
Phone: 061-317822 Fax: 061-317877 Email: hsi@iol.ie

PAPERBACK   ISBN 0 9538264 0 6
HARDBACK   ISBN 0 9538264 1 4

Printed and bound in Ireland by
Litho Press, Midleton, Co. Cork, Rep. of Ireland.

In the new Millennium, Sr Consilio was conferred with an Honorary Fellowship of the Faculty of Nursing and Midwifery at the Royal College of Surgeons, Ireland - an outstanding honour which she shares with, among others, Mother Teresa of Calcutta

DEDICATION

To my family

ACKNOWLEDGEMENTS

I am deeply indebted to all those who assisted in any way in the production of this book.

I am especially grateful to those who provided interviews, written material, valuable insights, time and patience.

To those who helped type and edit the manuscript, my sincere gratitude.

A special word of thanks to the members of the Cuan Mhuire family, past and present, for their impressions of the ethos which pervades the Cuan Mhuire movement.

Nora McNamara

FOREWORD

I am happy to have known Sr Consilio for many years. She reminds me of the Lord's words: "Be wise as serpents and simple as doves.". She has a profound simplicity and a faith which can move mountains and at the same time she is very much all there. To meet her, even for a short while, is to be invigorated and uplifted. The secret of Sister Consilio is love - a love based on the love of God and the unique worth of each person redeemed by the precious body of Christ. Our Lady plays a big part in this. Sr Consilio has a trust in Our Lady, which makes Mary's presence in Cuan Mhuire as real as it was in Nazareth. Sr Consilio's heart is as big as the ocean and yet she is no starry eyed enthusiast.

Twenty-five years ago when I became a Bishop, one of my Confirmation ceremonies was in the parish of Athy. After the ceremony, I visited the Convent of the Sisters of Mercy and there I met a wonderful group of nuns with an admirable Superior, Mother Mary of the Sacred Heart. Sister Consilio was in the group and I heard about her work dealing with drop-outs in the precincts of the convent. She then invited me up to see the first Cuan Mhuire, a few hundred yards up the road. I saw the whole area still in a rather primitive condition, with old sheds and outhouses, but I was immediately struck by the men and women in Cuan Mhuire, who were engaged in working on the place. They were obviously carrying out a labour of love and taking pride in their humble achievements. Sister Consilio introduced each one by name and told me what each one was doing and how well he or she was performing it. To me she was like someone talking to a member of her own family. And so I was captivated and captured by this extraordinary love and respect for each individual, and from then on I was privileged to enjoy the friendship of Sister Consilio and to help in the Blessing of the various foundations - all of which are described in this volume.

It is a record of events in modern Ireland, which can only gladden the hearts of Irish men and women everywhere, and remind us all that love and the grace of God can still be alive and flourishing in a world where materialism and selfishness may appear so dominant. Sister Consilio has many wonderful people helping her, including her own family, but her chief assistant is Our Lady, with whom she has a special line of communication, which never fails.

Most Reverend James Kavanagh DD

INTRODUCTION

I am pleased to tell you how this book came to be written.

Some years ago I broke my ankle; it was late at night and there was no chance of getting into a nursing home. In desperation I closed my eyes and said a prayer; immediately there flashed across my mind, Sister Agnes. I rang Sister Agnes and she said: "Come out Nora and we'll have a bed for you".

Sister Agnes who runs the Cuan Mhuire Rehabilitation Centre in Bruree, Co Limerick, is Sister Consilio's sister. They are cousins of mine, as our grandmothers; Johanna and Ellen Collins were sisters.

While in Bruree I had plenty of time to see the miracle that Cuan Mhuire is. I wrote his book, not only as a testimony to that miracle, but also as a tribute to Sr Consilio and her grandmother, the late Ellen Collins, who more than seventy years ago cared for my father when he suffered from the illness of alcoholism.

Nora McNamara.

CONTENTS

Chapter 1

THE EARLY YEARS

*"Jesus said: "My mother, and my brothers and sisters
are those who hear the word of God and put
it into practice."*

Eileen Fitzgerald, who would become better known by the title of
Sr Consilio of Cuan Mhuire fame, was born during a snowstorm on
the evening of January 9th 1937. She was called after her
Grandmother Ellen Guiney. She was the fifth child born to Maurice
and Mary Agnes Fitzgerald.

Maurice Fitzgerald was a farmer's son from Dromulton, Scartaglen,
in County Kerry. He was twenty four years of age when he met,
and fell in love with Mary Agnes Guiney, from Knockawinna, a
town-land four miles from the village of Brosna, on the Cork-Kerry
border. They were married in Brosna Church on St. Patrick's Day
1925.

Those were days when public holidays were scarce and when
every day, except Sunday, was a working day. The people worked
long hours and were content with what little they had. There was
no such thing as two weeks honeymoon for the newly-weds, so the
couple went off on a side-car for the day, returning that same
evening to be greeted by the music, dancing and "strawboys" of
the traditional country wedding.

Maurice and Mary Agnes set about building the family home at
Cloughvoula, and it was here that they would raise their family of
three boys and three girls.

Nowadays, Sr Consilio will talk of the wonderful parents with
whom she and her siblings were blessed. Indeed, the values which
she espouses today are, she will say, values which were nurtured
in the family home and which were passed on to her, and the other

family members. The world of her youth was a world in which honesty, gratitude, faith in God and Our Lady, and compassion for one's fellow human beings were instilled in the children.

Maurice Fitzgerald was a man possessed of a great sense of humour, a hearty laugh and a twinkle in his eye. Sr Consilio recalls his fondness for the simple pleasures of life - sitting by the blazing hearth fire and entertaining his children and "callers" with stories, jokes and poetry - some of which he composed himself. He loved the land which had been tilled by the Guineys for generations.

Every shrub, every tree, every blade of grass was precious in his sight. He believed that the task on hand was the "most important" task, so every task had to be done to perfection. This was obvious in the way he walked around the meadows, "clean-raking" them by hand, in the days before even the horse-drawn wheel rake or "Tumbling Paddy" was invented.

It was with the same care that the turf was cut and each sod laid by the next with precision. Maurice never needed an alarm clock - not even when he had to rise at two or three in the morning to walk his cattle to the fair in Abbeyfeale or Castleisland - a distance of some twelve miles.

To Maurice, the fairs were special, as was the daily trip to Mountcollins creamery, where there was always time for the "craic" with neighbours, and an exchange of news and views. On his way home from the creamery he would call to Billy O'Neill's shop for more "craic" and for the pound of raisins to make a currant cake for supper. No one smoked at home so he jokingly referred to the raisins as "our fags".

Maurice was a naturally protective parent and Sr Consilio recalls this aspect of his parenting: *"Looking back now, I know that my father, without making it obvious, was very protective of us and always kept an eye for each and every one of us. He made sure he always knew where we were and what we were about. He understood the world and all its pitfalls better than my mother. She saw only goodness in everyone. My father had a great insight into the dangers children could slip into."*

Maurice's wife, Mary Agnes was a handsome woman and she was the "heart and soul" of the household. She loved her home, her flowers, her hens, her geese, her collie dogs, but most of all the children with whom God had blessed her and Maurice. Both Mary Agnes and Maurice were welcoming people who had great time for neighbours and friends alike, and the kitchen of the family home was often filled with "ramblers", card-players and fiddlers. They were kind-hearted people who were often called on whenever their neighbours were in difficulty of one kind or another.

In those days, there were no vets in the area and Maurice was sent for, whenever a neighbour's animal was sick, or a pig needed to be killed. Maurice would take out his "Book of Cows and Horses" and, armed with the knowledge gleaned from its pages, he would hurry off to do all he could for the sick animal.

In a word, these were two people who knew how to give and take, and who passed on to their children that willingness to share and to help others. They were people who got down on their knees to pray before starting the day, and they again got down each night with their children to pray the family Rosary - theirs was a home in which the Family Rosary was recited every night of their fifty eight years of married life.

Undoubtedly, it is the "spirit" of her parents which hovers so close to Sr Consilio - their love and positive influences on her own life , which find echoes in so many of the situations enacted in the Cuan Mhuire houses; the compassion for others, the selfless acts of kindness and the simple act of just "being there" for the man or woman who needs help.

When Sr Consilio speaks of her parents, we might be simply listening to her talking the "Cuan Mhuire way" - as all the cherished values and virtues shine through: *"The year I spent at home after doing my Leaving Certificate was one of the happiest years of my life. My parents were extraordinary people. They gave us a lot of freedom and responsibility, and above all they showed us trust and love. It was just great waking up in the morning without a care in the world. I enjoyed the time with my parents. The joy of being able to be of some assistance to my mother who worked so hard, and in many ways I was able to help my father too. He was a man who loved company and*

3

encouraged me to give him a helping hand around the farm. As a child and a young girl I loved to walk with him through the fields and meadows near our home and around the barn, stable and cowhouse.

He was a brilliant storyteller and he had an unending supply of stories to tell - one better than the other. He preferred to talk about the pleasant things, and was always reluctant to discuss less pleasant issues. Whenever we mentioned things he would prefer not to hear about - things for which he felt there was no immediate solution, he would say 'we won't talk about it now - let the last half-hour be the hardest'."

Sr Consilio remembers her father as a man who made one feel they could not displease him. He never said a straight "no" to any request to go some place that he felt children would be better off not going, yet the man had a quiet, gentle way of dissuading his children from taking a particular course of action.

On one occasion, the young Eileen had been invited to go to the stations (i.e. Mass) in the house of a friend Mary, who lived a few miles from the Fitzgerald home. This was a custom for each townland in the area: *"When I made known my intentions, and in particular that I intended to go to Mary's house the night before the stations, no comment was passed. The night before my planned visit to Mary's, my father was going to do something for a neighbour's sick cow so he asked me to come along with him. On the way home he said to me 'I know that you're thinking of going to Mary's tomorrow night, but you know yourself how busy people are, and how much has to be done the night before the stations. Don't you think you would be as well to wait and go up in the morning and not be giving them extra trouble?' What could I say, even though I had plans made. My father didn't say so, but no doubt he knew that I had other plans for the night as well as going to Mary's!"*

There were other occasions when her father's concern for her well-being was demonstrated in a tactful but equally effective manner. The time, for instance, when young Eileen wanted to go to a "Wren Dance". These were dances run in various houses in the area and organised by groups of people who collected money 'hunting the wren' on St Stephen's Day. From the proceeds they bought lots of food and a few barrels of porter. The party went on from nine o'clock at night to seven or eight o'clock the following morning.

Sr Consilio remembers: *"My brother Johnny was going, so I waited my chance and when my father was on his way out to visit a neighbour's house, I went out in the yard after him and asked 'is it all right if I go with Johnny to the dance? He stood in the yard and looked at me with his usual kind smile and said 'you know how much I like to see you enjoying yourself, and nothing would please me more than to see you having a good time, but you know something, there will be an awful lot of old porter there, and maybe you would be as well off if you didn't go'. He didn't say there would be people intoxicated or anything like that - he just blamed the 'old porter'. What could I do with a father like that except stay at home? He had a way about him that always let you know you were loved and that you could make your own choices - but how could one disappoint him?*

He had a very strong sense of intuition. I always felt he could read my mind and, on this account, I always made sure not to think any thoughts in his presence that I knew he wouldn't agree with. There were many times when he could tell you ahead of time what was going to happen. Many years later, after I had joined the Nuns in Athy, I happened to be in Cork city unexpectedly and I decided to come home. When I arrived home at 2 a.m. I thought to myself: 'My parents will get a fright when they see me arriving at this hour of the night. 'I threw a stone up at the window, and when my father came down to open the door, he said: 'Do you know Eileen, I was expecting you, something told me you would come tonight.' Years earlier when I was training as a Nurse in Cork there were many occasions when I came home unannounced. I would get the bus to Newmarket and hire a bicycle to get home. I never once came home that I didn't meet my father down at the end of the road waiting for me. He told me in later years that the only time he waited for me and that I didn't arrive was the Christmas night after I joined the Sisters of Mercy in Athy. The strange thing was that when I left home to join the nuns I promised myself that I would come home at Christmas when I had my conscience satisfied, and when I had found out that I wasn't meant to be a nun. He must somehow or other have sensed that from me. When Christmas came I knew I was where I was meant to be and I didn't come home."

Eileen Fitzgerald continued to live at home with her parents after completing her Leaving Certificate. Her older sister Ita was by this time a member of the Sisters of Mercy in the Convent at Ardee, Co. Louth. Eileen would visit Ita occasionally and during one such visit, Ita asked her what she intended doing with her life. *"I was undecided whether I should go nursing or train to be a domestic science teacher. I had a real flair for cooking and housekeeping. When I asked my father for advice his answer was typical of the man: 'You should make up your own mind about it, it's your life, but I think you know enough about cooking, and if you went nursing you would be some use to someone'.*

I followed his advice and trained as a nurse in the North Infirmary Hospital in Cork. The hospital was run by The Daughters of Charity. They were a very dedicated group of nuns and a great inspiration to us trainee nurses. I will never forget their goodness to us and in particular their kindness to my own mother when she was very ill. At that time I was in the Noviceship and could not get permission to visit my mother. Sr Raphael Caffrey and Sr Agnes Monaghan did all they could to help my mother, and to make her stay in hospital as painless as possible."

The Sisters of Charity encouraged their nurses to do visitation of the sick or needy in Gurranabraher - a local housing estate. The nurses who chose to do so, went in pairs and were easily recognisable in their navy uniform coats. The Sisters of Charity provided the tea, sugar, butter etc which the nurses took to so many homes. This was in the late fifties and money was scarce. It was a time when trainee nurses received the princely sum of one pound and thirty pence per month; so they appreciated the fact that the bus conductors, aware of their mission, never took fares from them. Sr Consilio spent most of her off duty in Gurranabraher where she got to know and love the people. Years later when she was doing her midwifery in St. Finbarr's Hospital, Cork she was delighted to find herself once more in Gurranabraher - this time in the capacity of a midwife.

Sr Consilio says: *"I have no doubt today but that my father was right. He was a man with great insight."*She would come to rely on her father's intuition and insight in the difficult years ahead, when she decided to establish Cuan Mhuire, amidst all the self-doubt which beset her. *"Much later, when I struggled with so much opposition from all sides, and with so much uncertainty in my own mind as whether I should continue with Cuan Mhuire or not, I found myself constantly asking: 'Am I alright,' and 'am I doing the right thing?' One evening, I waited for my father to come home from seeing the cattle. I asked him* *what I should do. He said: 'Why are you asking me?' When I told him of my fears and in particular of the concerns of others, his reply was: "Take no notice of them, and if I am any judge, you will not go too far wrong."* He was quick to reassure young Eileen of full support from home, *"as he felt I would meet many others who would judge me and doubt my efforts."*

Maurice Fitzgerald prized truth and honesty. On one occasion, when a caller knocked on the door of the family home, Ita (Sr Agnes) who was at home at the time went to answer the knock. In spite of the difficulties her father had been having as a result of a stroke, she noticed him struggling to get up the stairs, supporting himself by putting two hands on each step of the stairs. When Ita asked her father why he had gone upstairs his reply was simple: "I thought that it was someone enquiring about Tom* (a family friend). I wouldn't want to give any information and I couldn't tell a lie, so I went upstairs" It was clear to the children that when their father told them that "no lie can be lawful or innocent" he was prepared to go to great extremes rather than tell the smallest untruth. During his lifetime, Maurice was often heard to say he had a fear of death - when death eventually came to him, in his eighty-fourth year, on October 7th, 1984 (The Feast of the Rosary) it came gently. He knew he was going to God and he went surrounded by his loving family, eleven months to the day after the death of his beloved wife Mary Agnes.

"My mother was a wonderful woman - so loving and full of care for everybody. She made us feel so special. She was always there to see us out to school each morning, and she was there in the evening to welcome us home with open arms. I scarcely went home from school of an evening that she did not hand me a message bag with maybe a cake of home-made bread, a bottle of milk, and very often a clean shirt, depending on whom I was visiting. She would say: "Run back to....with this bag and do not let anybody see you" - her left hand wasn't to know what her right hand was doing. She certainly made life better for a great many people. When anyone was sick in the locality she visited them, maybe staying at night and helping in every way she could. As children she had us making Novenas for the sick and troubled people she knew. Her

* Name changed

favourite Novena was The Rosary Novena which she said constantly in addition to the Family Rosary.When it came to doing something more difficult there was the Novena to Saint Jude. My sister Ita and I were sent every second Saturday to Brosna for Confession - this was part of the Novena to Saint Jude. We usually walked the eight miles return journey. As we got a little older, Ned - our next door neighbour, lent us his donkey and cart. On one occasion as we turned up Ahane cross we noticed a pedestrian directly in front of us. She was a very heavy, elderly lady and we were in a quandary. We felt it would be unfair to the lady to leave her walk the two miles to Brosna, and unfair to the donkey to give him the extra load. Finally, we decided that we would offer the lady a lift and that we would get out and help the donkey pull the cart. However, no sooner had the lady got up on the cart than Ned's donkey showed his objection by lying down on the road. We must have been a sight trying to pull the donkey back on his feet.

I remember coming home from school one evening and climbing up on a chair, hoping I would find a doll in the press. I had got the doll a few weeks before as a present. My mother asked me what I was looking for, and then said 'if you are looking for your doll, I gave her to a little girl who called here today. She hadn't a doll and you have had that doll for the past few weeks'. I remember getting down off the chair. I knew that my mother loved me because that was the kind of mother she was, but I also saw that she loved this little girl too. It was a lesson I never forgot. Years later, when I came in contact with people drinking wine, I thought: 'How would my mother feel if a brother of mine had ended up going from county home to county home with a bottle of wine in his pocket?' Then like the little girl down the road, I realised 'he' was my brother too, and that was the beginning of Cuan Mhuire."

Sr Consilio's mother was seventy years of age when the first Cuan Mhuire was started, and for the remaining nineteen years of her life she worked tirelessly for it. Visitors from Cuan Mhuire - no matter how many called - were always welcome in her home. She would rush to get the tablecloth and put a meal on the table. Her help did not stop there. She was eighty years of age when the first sale of work was held in The Devon Hotel, Templeglantine in aid of Cuan Mhuire, Bruree. Sr Agnes was organising the sale and needed helpers. Her mother enlisted the help of John Joe Curtin, the local postman. Here is part of the text of her letter to Sr Agnes concerning the matter:

Cloughvoula
October 10th, 1982

Dear Ita,

John, the postman called today. He said he hadn't heard from you so I gave him your phone number. He and three other men who are very good, are anxious to help you on Sunday. They are experienced; they look after the old folks' party and every celebration at Rockchapel. You will be very pleased with them. If you haven't already contacted them, do so. John does the post every day except Sunday, and he is home early from work. On Saturday he comes to evening Mass at the Rock. If he is not at home when you ring, his wife will take the message.

I am praying for your success,

Love from your Mother

Mary Agnes wasn't content with simply getting others to help - she helped out herself in every way possible. In May 1983 she expressed a wish to visit her relatives in County Limerick. She did so and spent a week in Cuan Mhuire, Bruree. Shortly after her return home she seemed tired. By October of that year she was obviously not well though she never complained.

On November 1st 1983 Sr Consilio went home to spend a few days with her parents. On the afternoon of November 2nd she was working in the garden when her mother called her. Sr Consilio said to her mother as she entered her room: *"I'm looking after the flowers so that they will be grand when you get up."* "Dear child," her mother replied, "I won't need the flowers anymore." Mary Agnes loved flowers all her life and her loss of interest in them was an indication of just how ill she was. Mary Agnes Fitzgerald died on November 6th 1983. She was surrounded by her family. She spoke to each child individually as they gathered around her bed, advising one not "to burn the candle at both ends, and not to catch cold through sitting near an open window," while to another she said: "I hope your work prospers." Maurice, who at the time was himself far from well, was in bed. Mary Agnes beckoned him from his bed because she had something of great importance to tell him. In what must have been the most poignant moment in the long love story that was this wonderful couple's lifelong union, Mary Agnes told her husband that she had earlier forgotten to tell him that if she were starting her life all over again, he was the man she would want to marry.

Cardinal Tomas O'Fiaich wrote the following letter to Sr. Consilio after hearing of her mother's death:

Ara Coeli
Ard Mhach/Armagh

5th January 1984.

Dear Sister Consilio,

I missed the death of your mother in the papers and did not hear of the sad event until recently. Please accept this note of sympathy, I know that a mother's departure is in many ways the saddest of all bereavements, and I pray that God will reward her with a place in His Kingdom, and give yourself and the other members of your family renewed strength and courage in these weeks of grief.

Wishing you every blessing in your work in 1984 and with an assurance of a remembrance of your mother in my prayers.

Very sincerely

Tomas O'Fiaich

Her funeral Mass was concelebrated at Knockaclarig Church by Fr O'Brien and Fr Dan Griffin of Brosna, Fr Butterfield of Carlow and Fr Herbert S.J. of Malta. In a tribute to Mrs Fitzgerald, Fr O'Brien said: "In death life has changed, not ended: we in faith would hope that life has changed for the better and in the case of Mary Agnes I am sure that is very true; that today she is as happy as she ever was on earth, and where she is gone we hope to follow. All of us in life are given many different tasks and her four main tasks were to be a good wife, a good mother, a good neighbour and a good friend. Those of you who knew her will say "ten out of ten" for Mary Agnes in those four tasks."

Mary Agnes Fitzgerald was laid to rest in Mountcollins Cemetery. Many of her friends including members of the Cuan Mhuire family, shouldered her coffin for the last half mile. Young and old shed a tear for the gracious, humble lady who always had a welcome for everyone and never let them leave without giving them something. Her last words were "Sweet Jesus come from Your Heavenly Home and show me Yourself how to die." She was 89 years of age.

Sr Consilio writes of her close neighbours: *"The word neighbour was a very familiar word in our house. So often I heard my mother telling people who called, about the great neighbours we had. There was our next-door neighbour Lily, who called every day when I was a child. Lily wasn't married at the time. I can remember how she used to take me to her house for my afternoon 'nap'. I can still remember how she lifted me on to the high bed and 'tucked' me in. Some years later Lily was married as was her brother Ned, so we had a new neighbour - Ned's wife May.*

I first met May the day she married Ned. She was a quiet and gentle lady. That night we danced our feet off as the music played and all the neighbours gathered to celebrate after the wedding and to welcome May into the neighbourhood. May was then, and is surely today, an answer to my mother's prayers. What a blessing it was for Ned to find such a precious wife, but it was also a blessing for us. The likes of May you could never meet. She is a rare kind of person; the only person I ever knew who never spoke unkindly or critically of anybody - a special gift no doubt! She has a great sense of humour and always avoids getting involved in any kind of disagreement."

Sr Consilio recalls how one night in her parents' latter years when they were sitting watching television in the company of May. *"My father said to my mother 'Mary, do you notice that all the people on television tonight are black people?' 'Not at all Mossie', my mother replied, 'they are all white'. When they couldn't come to an agreement on the colour of the people, my father called on May to solve the problem asking, 'May, what colour are they?'. May paused for a moment and then she said, 'Do you know, they are kind of red!' That answer really*

11

summed May up. As far as she was concerned neither was wrong!

May was always there during the year I spent at home after doing my Leaving Certificate. At night we visited the Dempseys - neighbours of ours who were as discreet as May herself. I confided all my secrets to May without the slightest fear that they would ever be revealed to anybody. May was certainly a great companion and friend to my mother. They were in and out to each other many times a day, sharing the news of the day and often the pastries they had made. My mother would have shared her worries, but May in her own silent way would never complain about anything. Like Our Lady, I believe, 'she treasured all things in her heart'. When my mother was dying she asked May to look after my father and Agnes. After my mother's death May moved into our house to look after my father for the last eleven months of his life and she has been looking after Agnes ever since. May certainly fulfilled her promise to my mother with a love and a care that could never be measured.

Nobody could replace my mother in my eyes but I have to say May has become a second mother to me. It's always a joy to go home to her. No matter how many I bring with me they get a hearty welcome. Even the beautiful brown bread and the currant cake my mother used to bake, May can turn out with equal perfection. Her presence has kept our home the same welcoming, warm place it always was. She is one in millions - a blessing from God and Our Lady who could never be replaced."

Sr Consilio recalls other neighbours and family friends - also with great affection: *"Peg Roche looked after me when my little sister Agnes was born. My father would lift me gently over the fence and into her arms each morning until such time as my mother was well enough to look after me. There were so many neighbours who showed me so much love as a child and helped set me out on life's journey believing that all people are good, and I clung to this belief all down the years - even though at times we have to search a little deeper to get in touch with this goodness."*

Sr Consilio remembers many happenings from those early days. There was the day when strangers were working in the house. The usual order was upset. Jumping suddenly from the fireside bench she knocked over the kettle that stood on the hearth, and she was badly scalded. Six year old Ita was angry with the nurse who came to dress Eileen's burns, because of the pain she was causing her little sister. This event, I feel, taught both of them something about the pain involved in healing.

There was yet another winter's day when Ita and Eileen decided to clean up the muddy cow tracks in a field with a brush and shovel, only to end up covered in mud themselves, having left their shoes stuck in the same mud.

When the time came for young Eileen to start school, Ita would take her by the hand down the long meadow and across the river Braonach to Knockaclarig National School. They were often accompanied by a lone pet sheep who would wait outside the schoolhouse all day and then return home with the two little girls at 3.30pm. Even at such a young age little Eileen had a charisma which drew people to her. Teresa O'Connor, one of Consilio's early teachers wrote of her young pupil in a letter to the author:

"Sr Consilio went through Primary School while I taught in Knockaclarig. I have a clear recollection of her first days at school even though I was not teaching juniors. She was a small, chubby little lady who had a very winning smile, dancing brown eyes and a head of brown curls. When she was in the middle classes - second, third, and fourth, she was still the same happy and very pleasant pupil who was helpful and a delight to teach. Learning was no problem to her as she was very intelligent. One duty she never neglected was to supply flowers from her mother's garden for the little altar to Our Lady on the classroom mantel piece. It is a great pleasure for me to relate my memories of her childhood in school, and to have lived to see her devote her life to bringing such happiness into the lives of others who are less fortunate."

The trips to and from school are recalled with fond memories by Sr Consilio. After school there were regular trips to Tado Curtin's shop for the "messages" and a copy of "Ireland's Own" for her father. On their way home Eileen and Ita would sing many songs - "The Garden Where the Praties Grow", "The Croppy Boy", or "The Rose of Tralee" - all to the same air... After tea, they played school - turning chairs upside down - each chair leg representing a student, and each chair leg getting its own quota of praise or punishment.

Looking back on her school days, Sr Consilio recollects: *"Mrs Moran was my first and best teacher. She was a woman of deep faith. I remember her preparing us for first Holy Communion. I can remember distinctly her talking to us about examining our consciences from deep down inside us. She gave me my first insight into the reality of my soul - for this I will be extremely grateful. She understood the true meaning of education as she called forth in each one of us the goodness and the giftedness that God has given us. She too understood how much our futures depended on how she helped us to make a good start on the journey of life.She had a special care for those who didn't have very much of this world's goods and made sure that her own children were not allowed to enjoy any privileges in school that were not given to the rest of us.*

Miss O'Donoghue, later to become Mrs O'Connor took over from Mrs Moran in second standard. She was much younger, very energetic and never accepted half measures. I always felt she had a soft spot for me. She was a brilliant teacher and prepared us well for the years ahead in school.

Master Kelleher taught us in the fifth and sixth classes. He was a great teacher and he taught us far in excess of the curriculum demands. I left Knockaclarig well equipped for secondary school."

The highlight of the school day was coming home through the fields in the evening with her head tucked under the tail of her brother Joe's coat. On a particularly wet evening her father would go to meet the children, and they would all fit under the tail of his big overcoat.

When Sr Consilio went to Secondary School at the Convent of Mercy in Abbeyfeale, she cycled into town from home every Monday morning. Her mother always put some money into her hand before she left the house. When she ran upstairs to say goodbye to her father, he would tell her to put her hand into his pocket and take out a half-crown for herself. The young secondary school student would rarely ask for money for herself. She bought her copy books and other school necessities out of her pocket money as she *'didn't want to be a burden to anybody'*. *I got on my bicycle about 6.30 a.m so as to catch up with some of my homework, which I had neglected to do at the weekend. The heavier the rain poured down on Monday morning the better I liked it. In school, if our clothes were wet, we were sent down to the boiler house to dry them; this meant we escaped class. There were many Monday mornings when I thought I was not wet enough to be sent to the boiler house. On those occasions I would get off at a well at the top of a hill in Killconlea and dip my skirt in the water to make sure it was so wet that I would be sent to the boiler house. I hated facing school on Monday mornings but when we were getting out at 3.30.pm I said 'the week is over'. I really didn't mind the rest of the week."*

One of her teachers, Sr Evangelist, remembers the young Eileen: "A face I remember well in St Joseph's Secondary School in Abbeyfeale is that of Eileen Fitzgerald now known as Sr Consilio of Cuan Mhuire, Athy. Her radiant smile and eager brown eyes, one could not forget.Humour radiated from her. Her talents were diverse, she was no small figure in poetic composition. Her ballads were tuneful comments on the topics of the time.

After her secondary education, she qualified as a nurse and then when God spoke to her, she listened. She undertook an enormous task. The vice of drunkenness is only too common today. It is a reminder of the broken condition of mankind in our world, not yet fully redeemed.

Sr Consilio realised there is no need to despair in the case of alcoholics who are willing to seek help. She has shown faith and hope in them, and she has built a "home from home" for them in the lovely grounds in Cardington, Athy. The object of this home is to give ill, depressed, and destitute people excellent care by way of food, comfort, rest, heat, and a recovery programme. Arresting their downward progress is the solution. Sr Consilio seeks no reward for her labour of love and hard service. "Blessed are the merciful, they shall obtain mercy." Her splendid work will live on in history. She is a wonderful Sister of Mercy of the 20th Century - one who commands respect throughout the nation and beyond it.

Sr Consilio recalls: *"As the journey was too long to cycle home every night I stayed during the week with my uncle and aunt - Mary and Bartholomew Guiney. They lived on a small farm three miles outside the town of Abbeyfeale. As they had no children of their own they lavished all their love and affection on me. It was surely a great place to be - there* was such peace and happiness. They had little of this world's goods but they had an abundance of goodness and harmony. Living there was a wonderful experience. It was the kind of house one loved to come home to. There was never the slightest hint of tension. Mary and Batt, as they were called, loved each other dearly; the only complaint I ever heard was when Mary thought Batt was smoking too many cigarettes for the good of his health. Yet, because she knew he couldn't manage without them, she gave me a packet for him every morning before I went to school. She hated cigarettes so much that she didn't want to be seen as condoning his actions. She must have had a premonition because some years later, Batt died from lung cancer - no doubt the cigarettes played their part in his last illness."

Mary and Batt had built a new house the year Eileen started school and there she was given the front room and a new bed. Until the day they died, they called it "Eileen's Room". Sr Consilio has only happy memories of this house and recalls how cosy and comfortable it was there. "I can never remember one unhappy moment in that house". The house was a focal point of fun and entertainment.

"As was customary at that time many of the local men called at night 'ag cuairteoireacht'. Aunt Mary knew that once they called and the story telling and fun began that would be the end of my homework, so she forbade them to come until 9.30 p.m. - Monday to Friday nights. At the dot of half past nine the latch was lifted. The fun we had was unbelievable. They had so many stories to tell, plus the news of the day. There were no televisions or radios and we didn't bother with the daily paper. At that time people were so important they got all the attention and a great welcome. They knew they were very important to Batt and Mary.

I remember going to the Listowel races. Ann* was a little girl who lived near my uncle's. Ann and myself booked two seats in what was then called a 'hackney car' - now known as a 'cab'. The 'hackney car' was bringing people to the races. I had planned to meet my brother Johnny in Listowel, and I hadn't mentioned to my parents that I was going to the races. We didn't go to watch the horses running, instead we stayed

---

* Name Changed

16

in the market-yard enjoying the bumpers, the chairoplanes, the swinging boats, the various and varied stalls, and the wheel of fortune. As planned, I met Johnny and he provided the money I needed to participate in all the fun. I won thirteen different prizes on the wheel of fortune - everything from china dogs, fancy delph and all kinds of ornaments. The last prize, a beautiful statue of the Little Flower - a saint I greatly admired for her simplicity and her endurance. It was great to win all these things, but how was I going to bring them home when I wasn't supposed to be at the races! I packed them into the boot of Sean Connor's car (the hackney driver) and asked him to leave them at Galvin's shop. I used to help Mrs Galvin to serve the customers after Mass on Sundays. I warned Sean to tell Mrs Galvin to say nothing about the prizes until I got home myself. But the warning fell on deaf ears! Worse still, one of the passengers in the car went for a few drinks too many and couldn't be found until quite late. Ann was panicking. She knew she would be in trouble if she were late home. I had to come through Sheehan's* yard on my way to my uncle's and as I hurried past I heard Mrs Sheehan saying to Ann: 'What kept you out until this hour of the night?' As I rounded the corner of the house she was calling me to come back and account for my movements but I ran as quickly as I could to my safe haven. When I told Mary and Batt what happened and how angry Mrs Sheehan seemed to be, Mary turned to Batt and said: 'Now wasn't I right not to let you go down to Sheehan's to meet Eileen, as I knew you would get the stick too.' The following morning when I called for Ann I got a terrible telling off and was blamed for Ann taking a loan of Mrs Sheehan's make up to brighten our faces for the races.

Every Friday night Mary went to visit Daisy Fitzgerald who lived just a few fields away. I went with her and played all sorts of games with Daisy's children. Afterwards we enjoyed her fresh griddle bread with butter steaming off of it, and homemade blackcurrant jam. Later when I was training as a nurse, I would come on holidays to Knocknasna. The boys who used to visit at night time planned that each one of them would ask to see me home from the dance in Abbeyfeale on a particular Sunday night. I wasn't aware of their plan. I met them and danced with each one of them. I hadn't the heart to put any one of them before the others so I suggested that we would all come home together, and so we did. All these have remained friends of mine down through the years. In

* Name Changed

those days life was so much simpler, relationships were life giving, beautiful and lasting with no aftertaste of being used or abused.

Coming home from school I left my bicycle in Jack McKenna's and crossed the footbridge to my uncle's as it was a few miles shorter than going around the road. Every evening Mrs McKenna gave me a cup of piping hot tea with lots of sugar in it. Strangely enough I never used sugar in my tea, but the cup I got from this very kind old lady had a taste all of its own. Whenever the river was high her husband or son Jack watched out for me from the gate, to see that I got safely across. The latch was always left off the door in the mornings so that I could step inside to change my shoes before collecting my bicycle in the shed. The concern, the care and the gentleness of these very special people who made me feel so welcome, so loved, and so important to them made a lasting impression on me during my whole life. 'Ni bheidh a leitheidi ann aris'.

After crossing the footbridge in the evening, I said the rosary, just as I did on my way to school in the morning - then as always since, Our Lady was, and is, my main support in life. I'd hate to think what could have happened to me without her guidance and constant support. Knocknasna has many happy memories for me. Auntie Mary was a rare kind of person - generous, big hearted, a great neighbour, a loyal and very special friend. She died on the Feast of Our Lady of Good Counsel in 1966. I have no doubt she is enjoying a well earned reward while continuing to look after those of us she left behind.

Batt was very shy and quiet, but very good humoured. He had the capacity to look at the bright side of every situation. He always was in good form and even in his last illness he didn't complain. He died as he lived - peacefully. Like Mary he had nothing to fear; he performed his work well without ever hurting or harming anybody. May their souls rest in peace.

There was Jack, Tom, Christy, Michael Browne and many more. If anyone was missing for a few nights there would be enquiries if they were sick, or if there was something wrong. Everyone felt important. As well as the many joyful things they had to tell, they also poured out any grief, sorrow or difficulties they were experiencing. No doubt it was group therapy at its best. For those who felt they needed to share a particularly difficult problem they waited to talk to Mary long after the rest of us had retired. What great lives they had!

There was an abundance of love, and all of these people felt seen, heard, accepted, and they certainly had a safe place to come to. Their needs were met. They had no need to go looking for 'professionals' to sort out their problems. What was happening at my uncle's home was happening in thousands of homes all over the country. People's basic needs were met in a very normal and homely situation. They felt needed and wanted; there was so much give and take it was just wonderful.

Unfortunately today the television - the box in the corner - is what is seen and heard in most homes. Children have to keep quiet because adults are watching programmes, and even worse still some children have their own televisions and they are exposed to material far beyond their years, and to programmes where violence, immorality and unrealistic living are the order of the day. To a child's mind these are all very real and normal; they actually believe to be true what they see on television. Their little minds are destroyed and tainted at a very young age and we see the result of it every day in the atrocities committed by our young people, mainly because we have failed to train and educate them and give them the dignity they deserve.

Young people need our time, our guidance and our love. They can do without many of their wants and much of the material goods they work themselves to death trying to provide, but they cannot become the beautiful people they are meant to be if they do not take care of their needs. I believe it is impossible for anyone, young or old, to read and watch violence and pornography without being adversely affected by it. Many people who commit serious crime, indulge in books, videos and programmes of this kind before becoming involved in crime."

Sr Consilio was also very close to her brothers and sisters. She recalls: *"Mossie is the eldest of our family, so my earliest recollections of him are as a teenager cycling to Mount Eagle school, and helping my father on the farm. He worked very hard as there was always so much to be done, and in those days there was very little machinery. At Christmas Santa brought me a pair of lovely shiny wellingtons - a real treat for me as now I could splash as much as I liked in every puddle and pool. With time the wellingtons got too tight, and I couldn't get them off by myself so I used to run to Mossie to pull them off - he always did so teasing that my leg could come off too!*

Mossie married Peggy Roche - our next door neighbour. My father always said he would do so as far back as when Peggy was going to the National School. They have eight beautiful children who have made, and are making, a great contribution to the work of Cuan Mhuire. Hopefully some of them will be there to help carry the work through long after we are gone. Mossie and home are synonymous. He was, and is, always there - a quiet hard working man - always responsible, caring and dependable.

When we were young my mother used to say about Johnny and myself, 'I never saw the beat of them!' They are like twins - you couldn't separate them!' Since I was a very small child Johnny, who was older than I was, took me under his wing. Whenever I had difficulties he sorted them out for me. He was very inventive. I remember him making a real sturdy wooden wheelbarrow with a wooden wheel. It lasted hauling stuff around the farm for years. He assembled his first bicycle from parts he gathered here and there, and he put a reflector off an old carbon lamp for a tail light. When he was going to school he used to knock down parts of the school wall so that the master would give him the job of building it during school time!! Johnny was, and is, a genius.

Later on when I was doing my Leaving Certificate, if I failed to work out one of my algebra problems Johnny could always come up with the answer even though he never learned algebra. He cut turf and turned "taobhfhods" for potato sowing at a rate that very few could compete with. The school master always insisted he should qualify as an engineer but Johnny had no interest in books. He worked it all out in practice. He spent some years in England building bridges and other such work but his love for farming and cattle brought him back home.

When it was decided to form The Cuan Mhuire Trust I asked Johnny to become a Trustee as I felt he would understand me and what I had to do, better than anybody else would. I knew he had a broad mind, a big heart, a deep faith, and that he would not be afraid to take risks. I also knew that he had the ability to look at the bright side of life and that he had an abundance of compassion. I knew too that he never counted the cost of something that needed to be done.

I'll always remember when I was very young, my father gave each of my brothers a calf. When Johnny sold his calf he put the money in an old cocoa box. *He brought me down to the stable and got me to climb up to where he had hidden his money saying 'that is where my money is, and if you ever want anything out of it, you can come and get it here'. That pattern continued down through the years and to this present day. He never ceases to amaze me, not just with money or material things but with years of hard work and total dedication and commitment to Cuan Mhuire."*

For many years now, Sr Consilio has relied on Johnny for so much of the building and development work of the Cuan Mhuire houses. He built a magnificent Cuan Mhuire complex at Athy and he carried out a total reconstruction of Bruree House, and Cuan Mhuire, Coolarne. Sr Consilio is in no doubt about the debt both she and Cuan Mhuire owe to him. *"I would be lost without him, and without him it would be impossible to have the beautiful centres that he has built with the help of our Cuan Mhuire Family. The buildings are monuments to him, and to them and they provide first class accommodation, treatment and recreational facilities for hundreds of people who would literally have no other place to go.*

Johnny is very shy, always taking a back seat when it comes to 'opening days' or other celebrations. He is a very successful farmer even though he has devoted so much time to Cuan Mhuire. He still has the energy to keep his farm going. He loves shooting and hunting. It is his main past time at weekends apart from visiting his neighbours and meeting them at the local pub on Friday nights. Like my father, he has a great capacity for storytelling and for seeing the 'silver lining' in the darkest hours."

Another brother Joe is also close to Sr Consilio's heart. According to her, *"Joe was always very gentle."* He too was always very protective towards his younger sisters, and Sr Consilio relates a story to illustrate the point: *"Once when I was about five years of age Joe told my mother he was too sick to go to school so I asked to stay at home with him. About 10 a.m. he was 'better' and we were both asked to tidy up oats which my father had thrashed. There was a big broken mirror beside the oats, and when I slipped, it went right through my thigh. Joe was very resourceful; he tore up one of the sheets from his bed, and bandaged my leg so tightly that he managed to stop the bleeding, even though the cut was very deep and about four inches long. He helped me to school the following morning but when Mrs Moran called me to her table I was unable to get off the desk, so she had to arrange for* me to be brought home. That was the first my mother knew about the accident.

Another time a friend of ours came visiting in a donkey and cart. When the visitor had gone to Brosna with my mother, Joe decided he would bring me up the road for a drive in the visitor's donkey and cart. On our way back, the donkey was going at such a speed with the fall of ground that when he came to turn in our passageway the bend was too sharp and the wheel hit the ditch. I heard Joe moaning on the ground while I held on for dear life, cocked up as I was on the seat and guards. For a minute I thought Joe was putting on an act in case I was hurt, but when I scrambled down he was rolling on the ground, doubled up with pain. After a while I helped him to his feet and brought him home. I stood in front of him until he went to bed later on. I was hiding him so that my father would not notice he was in pain. Of course the following morning he couldn't move; the fat was in the fire, and it was discovered he had several broken ribs. As children we had a code among us that there were no tales told.

Joe never lost his sense of fun, good humour and generosity. Years later I saw him amuse and play with his own son Gerard just like he did years ago with his younger sisters. In winter time when there isn't very much to do on the farm he always volunteers to help me in Cuan Mhuire.

Ita was the first girl in the family. Having started life playing with her three brothers may have accounted for the fact that she was very daring and never seemed to take danger into account. As a result she had many accidents, most of which were hidden from our parents. One of my first memories of Ita was when she was playing 'hide and go seek' in the hay barn. I must have been about three years of age as I was just standing there, too young to participate in the game. I saw Ita jump from the very top of the hay barn right down to the ground, in order to get to the 'den' before Johnny who was jumping from bench to bench to get to the ground. My brothers lifted her up unconscious. After sometime, and a lot of cold water, they managed to revive her.

Another day she slipped off a fence and an iron went through her stomach. On yet another occasion she injured her ear when she fell out of the horse's cart. Years later when she came home from school in England, she was describing a trap for catching animals, which she had seen in a British museum. My father said jokingly that he couldn't believe she had seen it without walking into it, as she had always 'walked into everything'. From her childhood she was very loyal and faithful. I remember her bringing me to school. We made lots of journeys together, and we continued to do so later on in life.

Ita grew up to be very artistic. She was excellent at all kinds of crafts and decorated our house with handwork. She went to secondary school for two years to Colaiste Mhuire (or Miss Woulfe's) as it was known, in Abbeyfeale, and then to England for a further three years. This meant we were apart a lot for five years. Fortunately, she spent a year at home before joining the Sisters of Mercy in Ardee, County Louth in March 1952. This gave us time together. When Cuan Mhuire started Sr Agnes (as Ita was subsequently known) worried a lot about the difficulties I got myself into. Looking back now I can understand how well founded her anxieties were, but in spite of her concerns she helped me from the very beginning in every way she could. At a time when money was very scarce and badly needed she worked so hard to raise funds through sales , raffles etc.

Seventeen years ago she agreed to come to Bruree for a year to help me out. That year has continued ever since. She has done trojan work in developing Cuan Mhuire Bruree and looking after the thousands of people who have passed through the centre. Agnes is a very hard worker; she never thinks of herself. Her commitment and dedication to Cuan Mhuire could not be measured. She has been, and still is, a tower of strength to me, ever loyal, ever faithful, always encouraging and supporting. Even the times when I fail to measure up she is always there helping me out, never condemning. I am truly blessed and very grateful for having such a wonderful, compassionate, and caring sister not just to me, but to all who come through our doors.

Unlike me, Sr Agnes had a flair for study and teaching She was quick to see the need for a training centre for Cuan Mhuire's Counsellors. Out of this insight grew the Two Year Diploma Course in Counselling at Galilee House of Studies, Athy, County Kildare which was initiated in 1992. Providing our own counselling course has added a very important dimension to the work of Cuan Mhuire. Furthermore, it has attracted a number of people who have themselves made a good recovery from addiction, have long term sobriety and feel called to work in the field of addiction. Without Sr Agnes this would never have been possible. I marvel how she manages to devote so much time to this work in spite of

23

all her commitments in Bruree. I suppose it is back to the old story of - if you want something done 'ask a busy person'. Sr Agnes has a great sense of humour and can tell stories just like my father used to do. The strangest and most unusual situation always keep cropping up for her so she is never short of material for creating a good laugh at anytime. Cuan Mhuire is definitely a richer and a better place because of her presence and her hard work. Long may she continue to be with us.

My first memories of my little sister Agnes are of the day she was baptised. I was three years of age at the time. I remember Lily, our next door neighbour had her all wrapped up in a beautiful white shawl after returning from the church. The taxi man brought me a huge bag of sweets and I was swaggering around the kitchen shaking them back and forth when one of my brothers pulled the corner off the bag, and then went about mending it. In the process he packed lots of paper into the bag and removed most of the sweets for himself and the others.

As time went on we began to notice that Agnes could not walk or talk like the rest of us; she was handicapped. I was always aware that my mother worried about her and brought her to many doctors in the hope of getting help for her. She also prayed for her night and day and asked Ita and myself to make Novenas for her. These entailed going to Holy Communion nine Sundays in succession. At that time a person who received Holy Communion every Sunday had to go to Confession every two weeks. We lived about four miles from the village of Brosna and we used to set out walking every second Saturday morning to get Confession in Brosna. At the time it may not have appeared that these prayers were heard but today I can see how every one of them was answered in God's own time.

Her life affected mine in many ways. Once she was able to get out and about I brought her with me everywhere I was going. In school she had the free run of the place, and when I was in fifth and sixth standard she used to come and sit beside me. Whenever I got slapped for not having my homework done, she cried. One day she called the master 'Darbie' - a name the pupils called him behind his back. He was very annoyed and blamed me. Agnes always brought the best out in all of us. I stayed on an extra year in primary school just to be with her. We made our Confirmation together in Brosna Church on May 16th 1950.

On one occasion a visitor to our house sympathized with my father because Agnes wasn't like the rest of us. My father's answer was 'aren't we blessed we didn't have a film star, if we had, we would never be finished worrying about her.' He always referred to Agnes as 'our own little saint'. That is what she is, and she has brought untold blessings on our house. She gave us, at a very young age, an understanding of the fact that there is a lot more to each one of us than what we do or what we achieve. If it weren't so, her life would be meaningless. Later on when I thought about joining the nuns I wondered should I stay at home and look after Agnes, but somehow I knew that if I did the best I could for others, God would look after Agnes. My parents cared for Agnes all their lives. She got first place at the head of the table, and when my mother died, May, who became a second mother to all of us, came to live in our house to take care of Agnes. Then I really saw how all my mother's prayers were, and are still, being answered today."

Sr Consilio's Parents - Mary Agnes & Maurice Fitzgerald

Sr Agnes (left) & Sr Consilio with their parents

Sr Consilio's Grandmother - Ellen Guiney (née Collins)

Sr Consilio's Home

Eileen Fitzgerald

Ita Fitzgerald

Ita (left) & Eileen Fitzgerald

Sr Consilio and her Father
-Taken in Cork City

Sr Agnes & her mother (aged 89 years)
- Taken during her last visit to Cuan Mhuire in 1983

Knockaclarig NS

Sr Consilio's First Teacher
- Mrs Eilish Moran

Mrs T. O'Connor (née O'Donoghue)

Master Kelleher

Sr Consilio's next door neighbour
- Lily O'Connor (née Guiney)

Convent of Mercy, Abbeyfeale, Co Limerick

Sr Ignatius

Sr Louis

Sr Evangelist

Sr Joseph

Some School Companies - Sr Consilio (centre, front row)

Sr Consilio's Aunt Mary

Sr Consilio's Uncle Batt

Sr Consilio, Sr Agnes & Mary Guiney

Sr Consilio's Brother - Joe, with Wife Philomena & Son Gerard

Sr Consilio and her Brother, Johnny

Sr Consilio's brother, Mossie with his wife Peggy, their eight children & son in law, Paudie Boland

Sr Consilio & her friend Mary Daly

Sr Consilio's neighbour
- Peg Roche

Sr Consilio at St Finbarr's
Hospital, Cork

Group taken at the North Infirmary Hospital Cork
Sr Consilio (4th from left, Back Row)

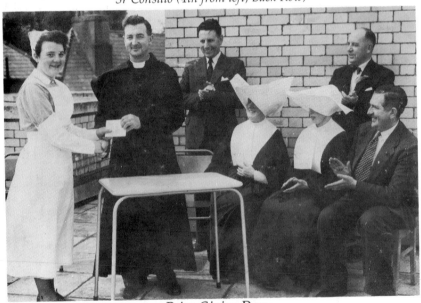

Prize Giving Day
- North Infirmary Hospital, Cork

Genogram

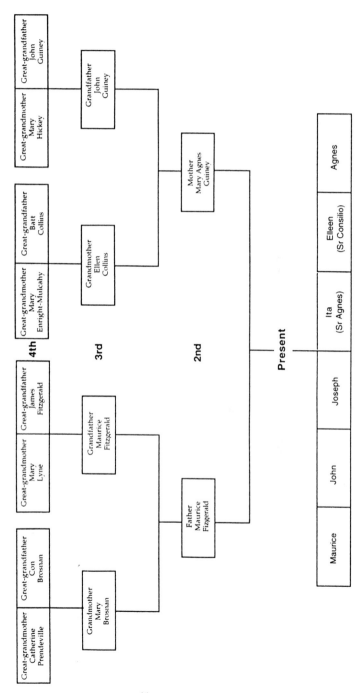

Chapter 2

ANSWERING THE CALL

*"Jesus went out and saw a tax collector
named Levi, seated at his post.
He said to him: 'Follow me'.
Leaving all, he arose and followed Him."*

Matthew 9, 9.

Whether at home, or at work, or at a dance, Consilio says she was always conscious that one day she would become a nun. It was not that she relished the idea - but simply that it was something she was convinced she couldn't get away from. Upon completion of her training as a nurse, Sr Consilio took steps to answer the call. She wanted to join an order that would allow her to go home to her parents if they were ill or needed her, but she also wanted to be some distance from her Kerry home and from Ardee, where her sister, Sr Agnes, was a nun. She felt this would spare them embarrassment if she ever stepped out of line!

Sr Agnes had heard how the Athy community of the Mercy Order was very welcoming and that there was a Sr Dominic there with whom she "could not imagine anyone being unhappy".This swung things for Sr Consilio and on 8th September 1959 she entered the Sisters of Mercy in Athy, Co. Kildare - a day, she says, she will never forget, as *"I felt my heart would break with loneliness"*.

Sr Consilio's brother, Johnny, took her to the railway station at Mallow, for the long, lonely journey to Athy. She would not allow him, or anyone else, to travel all the way with her as she felt she would be too lonely to part with them when they reached Athy. Johnny, seeing how upset his sister was, tried to persuade her to return home with him. He volunteered the opinion that she was "never meant to go". However, Sr Consilio reasoned that the nuns would be waiting to meet her in Portlaoise and that when she had "satisfied her conscience" she would return home for Christmas. Once there, however, Sr Consilio says she never thought about coming home again. She knew, beyond a doubt, that she was where she was meant to be.

The life of a novice in the late 50's and early 60's was a demanding one - especially for a person who was "free and easy". There was the maxim "Keep the Rule and the Rule will Keep You" and the time spent in the novitiate was seen as a time of "testing". The all-weather black habit, the long serge skirt, heavy woollen petticoat, wide detachable sleeves, big black pocket complete with pin cushion and tied about the waist, was one way of testing the novice. The complicated, starched headgear was another trial. They were uncomfortable to work with, but they were only the "externals" and Sr Consilio adjusted to them quickly. The inner change was not so easily made. There was much more to the training. Novitiates trained young women for a life of dedication and commitment - something Sr Consilio came to appreciate as the years went by. The daily 'examination' of conscience involved sitting on a little stool for twenty minutes every day. A little black notebook would be taken out and she would consider her faults and how she was dealing with them. Day after day she put a few marks here and there in the little book to indicate her spiritual progress. One day it dawned on the young novice that - whatever her failings - she was really doing nothing about them and that she was "making no progress" with herself. But there was one thing she could do, which was that she could love people more and more. From that day on, she made up her mind to be attentive to only one thing and that is to love every person she met. She said to herself *"I'll leave my failings behind me: I'll leave them sitting somewhere and I'll be so busy living out of my love, that they'll be pushed out bit by bit!"*

As a postulant, Sr Consilio taught second standard in the Primary School and she came to love the children there. Her first year as a "white veil" was a "Spiritual Year". As the term suggests, this year was meant to be a time of quiet and prayer and did not allow for any other commitment. It was the most important rung on the novitiate ladder - a period of intense spiritual formation. During the Spiritual Year novices studied the writings of the Spaniard, Rodriguez. He strongly advocated vowed obedience and acclaimed, for example, as a model, the novice who "planted cabbages upside down because his superiors told him to do so".

A far cry from Sr Consilio's down to earth, practical home training. Novices walked in the garden wrapped in woollen shawls while saying the Rosary. On one such occasion, Consilio had her spiritual reading book tucked under her arm. For convenience, she placed it on a stone under the nearby hedge and proceeded to forget about it. Some hours later, the novice mistress asked the assembled novices which one of them had left the book "The Nun, Her Character and Her Work" in the garden - no answer. Again the question was put and again it drew silence. The question was put a third time but now it was directed at Sr Consilio, who blurted out, *"Oh, I thought I had 'My Yoke is Sweet'."* History does record that her "yoke" was too sweet for the remainder of that evening! Apart from the spiritual, there was much that was special for Sr Consilio in that particular year. She was infirmarian and spent much of her time with the sick and elderly Sisters, whom she found to be a real inspiration and with whom she formed a genuine bond. Very often, in later years, when faced with difficulties of one kind or another, she returned to those elderly Sisters to ask for their prayers and advice. Years later too, neither time nor distance stood in the way of her getting to these sick Sisters when they were ill or dying.

In the second year of her novitiate she taught infant boys and fifth standard. She also got her first taste of work in St. Vincent's Hospital, Athy - an experience which she enjoyed and benefited from. *"The Matron, Sr Dominic is the person who was responsible for my joining the Sisters of Mercy in Athy. She is the nun about whom it was said: 'You couldn't imagine anyone being unhappy living in the same house as she was.' How right this was. Sr Dominic was full of fun and good humour, one of the most life-giving people I have ever come across. I met her on my first ever visit to the Convent in Athy. I took one look at her and I decided that this is the place for me. The whole atmosphere in St Vincent's reflected her big heart, her generosity, her homeliness and her deep insight into the needs of all patients, nurses, general workers and sisters. Everyone loved Sr Dominic and why wouldn't they. She was never off duty even when she had gone to bed, as the phone was always ringing, and she was forever on call. She had an answer for every problem that cropped up. In her own room you saw* little of her own goods, but it was stocked with all kinds of bits and pieces that she was trying to keep aside until they were required in different parts of the house. Times were very much poorer then regarding material things, but so much richer with love, understanding, concern and care for people. There were three hundred and twenty people in the hospital at that time. She knew every one of them by name."

Sr Dominic was obviously a major influence on Sr Consilio's life. "She never came to her meals without something amazing to tell. One cold morning she had put on a white woollen cardigan. A lady who had come for a night's lodging the night before, way-laid Sr Dominic on her way to breakfast, to complain that her own breakfast wasn't good enough. After lodging her complaint she said: 'Nuns - heaps of mate wrapped up in wool is all ye are!'. Sr Dominic ran the hospital always considering the poor and needy. She could get more done with one hundred pounds than others could with thousands. When Christmas came Sr Dominic managed to have a little gift for everyone". A custom that Sr Consilio preserves to this very day despite the hundreds of people who are now in her centres at any given Christmas.

Sr Dominic was always concerned that Sr Consilio might, through her relative inexperience, fall into "traps". One such trap is recalled by Sr Consilio:"Tom* had convinced me that he was going to England to get a job. I got money from home for his fare to England and I asked friends of mine to bring him good clothes. I bought his rail ticket and gave him pocket money. I also gave him a Rosary beads to keep him safe. All this unknown to Sr Dominic - so I thought! A few hours after he had supposedly left for England, word came that Tom had called into the convent very intoxicated, that he was very abusive and had thrown flower pots around the place. The nuns called the Gardai who showed no mercy to Tom. I said nothing but I knew the 'fat was in the fire'. The next morning, Sister Dominic smiled and told me word for word what I had done for Tom. She knew exactly what was happening. She never said: 'I told you so' - a quality I always admired in her. Neither did she tell those in the convent that I was the root cause of all the trouble. I was only a novice at the time, and would have been in serious trouble if the truth were known."

*Name changed

"Sr Dominic, was 'nobody's fool'. One evening the Gardai arrived at the hospital door. They lifted Danny* into the front hall and onto a couch. They had found him unconscious by the side of the road and could hardly lift him. To their embarrassment, Sr Dominic walked over to him and said: 'Get up out of that and go to bed, Danny boy.' He jumped up instantly and ran past the guards to his room. She could read him like a book. I remember her many times warning me in an effort to protect me from pitfalls.

Sr Dominic was such a mother to us all, and she never spared herself herself as she reached out to help not only those in the hospital, but many others who sought her advice and guidance in so many ways. Whenever she got ill, we all worried in case anything night happen to her.

Today, she is hale and hearty, even though she is now over eighty years of age. She hasn't changed a bit. Her big heart and good humour are still to the fore. I have no doubt her many prayers have helped me over the years, and maybe some day I will be able to do something for her in return."

*Name changed

Sisters of Mercy, Athy, Co Kildare

48

Convent of Mercy, Athy, Co Kildare

St Vincent's Hospital, Athy

Sr Dominic McHugh

Sr Peig Rice

St Vincent's Hospital, Athy: *the Little House at the end of the Garden*

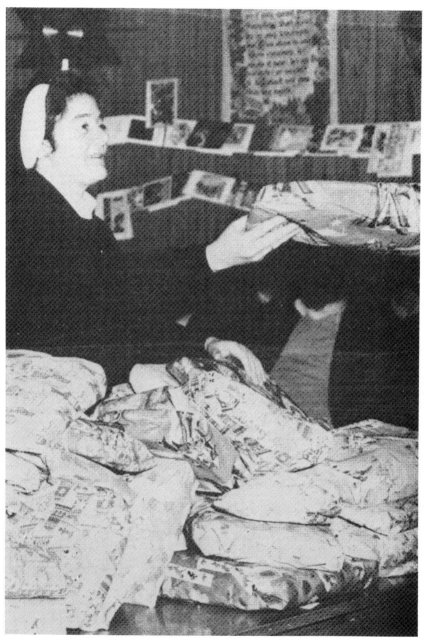

Christmas in Cuan Mhuire : Each Resident is given a gift

Chapter 3

CUAN MHUIRE - THE SEED IS SOWN

"For now we see in a mirror, dimly, but then we will see, face to face. Now I know only in part: then I will know fully, even as I have been fully known. And now faith, hope and love abide, these three: and the greatest of these is love."

1 Cor. 13

A fire broke out in a house in which a man was fast asleep. They tried to carry him out through the window. No success. They tried to carry him out through the door. No success. He was just too huge and heavy. They were getting desperate until someone suggested. "Wake him up, then he'll get out by himself!"

If Cuan Mhuire has come to mean different things to different people, one precept remains constant, unchanging and true - it is the underlying truth of God's love for every human being ever born and to be born. Sr Consilio is relentless in her quest to "wake" people up to the reality of their uniqueness and their capacity for spiritual growth. Cuan Mhuire provides the tools with which the addicted person will learn to fashion and to sustain and nurture his or her recovery. But always, the catalyst is the in-depth and unconditional love shown to each and every man and woman who seeks refuge within its walls.

The programme for recovery is a spiritual one - and how could it be otherwise? To come to a realisation of one's own personal worth, and one's uniqueness as a priceless human being is to be transformed. To discover that so much of one's progress depends on one's own attitude, is to see, perhaps for the first time in one's life, that a change in attitude can be a giant leap forward on the road back to life.

There was no "programme for recovery" in the early days. There was one little nun with a big heart and an abundance of courage and tenacity. A young woman who would find many obstacles in the way - the greatest of which, in the beginning, was self-doubt.

"When I struggled with so much uncertainty in my own mind, and so much opposition from all sides as to whether I should continue with Cuan Mhuire or not, I found myself constantly asking: 'Am I alright?' and 'Am I doing the right thing?'"

Life in the convent has changed - perhaps out of all recognition - since the days when Sr Consilio first donned the habit of a Mercy nun. Blind obedience was the order of the day. The Superior was always right.

That Sr Consilio had the courage and the faith to challenge that tradition says much for the love and compassion which motivated her in her decision to establish a permanent "home" for those in need of sanctuary. There are few who, like Sr Consilio, have been able to question one aspect of tradition without threatening its essence. Gandhi once said: "If I discovered, if somebody tried to prove to me that the "untouchables" are part of the real tradition of Hinduism, I would revolt against it." Mahatma Gandhi went to the "extreme" (as other Hindus saw it) of adopting an untouchable girl, of working in jobs reserved to the untouchables - the cleaning of latrines every day. He came to identify himself with the untouchables in such a way that he spent many weeks living with them, whenever he visited the cities. Politicians and diplomats who wanted to see him found him in the poorest areas where the untouchables, the "lepers" of India, lived.

And yet he was capable of questioning one aspect of tradition without doubting the whole tradition. For, of course, as Sr Consilio has put it: *"The most important thing in the whole wide world is love."*

> "Whoever welcomes you, welcomes me,
> and whoever welcomes me, welcomes the
> One who sent me."
>
> Matthew 10:40

During her time working in St Vincent's Hospital, Athy, Sr Consilio would come in contact with, and befriend, many "road men" - those men of no fixed abode who went from county home to county home, and found temporary lodgings in a little house at the bottom of the garden at St. Vincent's. They got their meals at a side table in the main dining room. She would come to know these men well from her work in the kitchen; she also looked after their sleeping accommodation and chatted with them at night time.

"I was interested in them and found them to be intelligent, often well educated people. Some of them had even changed their names as they didn't want to be recognised - they were so ashamed of their lifestyle. I often talked to them about their families and encouraged them to write home, particularly if their mothers were alive. I often thought how my mother would worry if a brother of mine were in a similar situation. As time went on I began to realise more and more that these people were my brothers, and I said to myself: 'Some day, somewhere, somehow, I will have a place that these people can call home'."

Sr Consilio knew, as she ministered to these wandering souls that they needed somewhere warm and dry, and welcoming, somewhere to return to at the end of the day, someone to show them love and compassion - all the comforts which are taken for granted by so many. *"It took me many years to discover that the person they most needed to love was themselves. By 'love', I mean seeing what is best in oneself."*

Sr Consilio would resolve to learn all she could about the scourge of alcoholism. She could see that alcohol was the road man's anaesthetic. If pain could be numbed, albeit temporarily, then most of these men would reach for the painkiller and many of them would go to their graves without ever having come to know themselves for the beautiful and unique human beings they were.

Sr Consilio attended her first open meeting of Alcoholics Anonymous in Carlow. She knew very little about alcoholism at this time. Her experience of the drink was a very limited one.

"The only thing I knew about drink was what I learned as a child when a cousin of ours used to contact my parents when he went on a 'binge'. My father would collect him in the pony and trap and bring him home

to us where he would stay for about six weeks. My mother weaned him off the drink with bottles of stout. Then she would send me along with him everywhere he was going, explaining to me that his sight was not too good. Now I know she understood he could not enter a pub while I was with him!"

Long before Sr Consilio was born, her grandmother did exactly the same for the author's father - Dr. Michael Joe Aherne. He was a dispensary doctor in Brosna, a small village eight miles from the town of Abbeyfeale in County Limerick.

His mother died when he was only two years of age so he saw his aunt Ellen Guiney (Sr Consilio's grandmother) as his second mother.

Shortly after he qualified and took over his father's practice in Brosna, it became obvious that he had a problem with alcohol. This was very serious, and he would no doubt have lost his practice on more than one occasion were it not for his aunt Ellen who would engage a locum, and take him over to the Guiney farm in Knockawinna where she cared for him until he got well. In a sense then, it could be said that my father was their family's first alcoholic.

Paddy Lambe will always be remembered for his part in setting up the original Cuan Mhuire. Sr Consilio first met him at an open AA meeting which he had organised in Carlow. He was quick to realise that she had a keen interest in those suffering from addiction. He began calling to her at the convent and soon he asked her to visit a few families who were experiencing difficulties due to alcoholism.

Paddy valued the attentive ear which Sr Consilio always gave him. He told her of others, who were in great need of someone to listen to their problems, and so there began the visits to see "the little nun" in the convent of Athy. Sr Consilio recollects that: *"Paddy and his wife Anne were extremely generous, caring people who were always ready to reach out a helping hand to others. Indeed, I often saw Anne bring boxes of groceries to families who needed them. Neither Paddy nor Anne spared themselves in those early days. They always helped at any hour of the day or night, despite the fact that they were very busy running their own business in the town of Athy. As I look back now, I realise how lucky I was to have a man of Paddy's calibre to watch out for me, at a time when I believed that everyone wanted only what was best for everyone else. It took me a long time to understand that this is not always so.*

Years later, Paddy told me that my father had asked him, in those very early times, to look out for me. Anne died while still young and just one year later Paddy died suddenly. Up to his death, he gave of his time to Cuan Mhuire. He will always be remembered as one of our founder members - one of our best friends, who never wavered in good times or hard times. He was loyal and faithful to the end. I pray that Our Lady and the Good Lord will reward Anne and Paddy for their great goodness and generosity to Cuan Mhuire."

Sr Consilio was never so busy that she could not stop for a little while and listen to the men and women who came to pour out their troubles to one who was prepared to listen. They tried at night-time not to make any noise but as "night silence" began in the convent at 9.00 p.m. it was inevitable that they would disturb the silence. *"Of course I got myself into all kinds of trouble!"* she says of this early period in her ministering to the road men.

After some time, Sr Consilio got the use of a music room located just inside the convent gate. The electrician who worked in the convent put in an electric socket for her. At least now she could go out and buy a kettle and some delph so that she could make a cup of tea for the visitors. She remembers collecting cards from Surf washing powder boxes in the hope of winning a prize to pay for these items. She won - and these things were paid for. During her time in the kitchen, Sr Consilio would bake some apple tarts, so there was always something for "the visitors", who often came very late and stayed for a long time - so great was their dread of the long, lonely nights.

Far too easily might it be forgotten, that these men and women were the rejects and outcasts of society - the untouchables for whom the joy and beauty of life had become a faint memory. To hold out the hand of friendship, to be attentive to their worries and concerns, and to see in each one a person of great dignity and value, would in turn have a transforming effect on many of those forgotten souls. It were as though Sr Consilio held a mirror up to the person, and, telling him time and time again how priceless he was in God's eyes, and in hers, he began slowly, to see himself for the beautiful person that he was.

"To my amazement, many of these people began to get sober through their sharing, through the fellowship and the friendship we experienced in that tiny little room."

The men and women in recovery invited Sr Consilio to attend their "open" AA meetings on Wednesday nights at the Cistercian Abbey in Moone, Co Kildare. Sr Consilio recalls the transformation she underwent during this time. *"I learned a lot from those meetings and followed as best I could, the A.A. way of life and found it very helpful. I made my meditation out of parts of 'The Big Book' from 6.30 am to 7 am every morning."*

All of these developments would bring with them their own problems, not least of which was the lack of space, as word spread along the "grapevine" of the dispossessed, that there is a "little nun" up in Athy who wants to help.

Dr Michael Joe Aherne & his wife Nora
Dr Aherne served as Medical Officer in the 1st World War

Paddy Lambe

Harry Goode

Sr Consilio & Liam Tiernan

Chapter 4

THE DAIRY

"For you have delivered my soul from death
and my feet from falling,
so that I may walk before God
in the light of life."

Psalm 56

Few parables in the New Testament are as moving or as inspirational as that of the Good Samaritan. Indeed, few are as blunt in terms of the message Christ seeks to convey. When posed the question: "Who is my neighbour?"Christ responds with his parable of the traveller who is attacked and stripped by robbers, on the road between Jerusalem and Jericho. The priest and the Levite were travelling on the same road, but each of them "saw him and passed by on the other side." The Samaritan, on the other hand, "saw him, and had compassion on him". Even as he departed the scene, he entrusted the poor man to the care of a local innkeeper, promising to pay any expenses incurred by the innkeeper.

No Christian can be left in any doubt as to what our relationship must be to our suffering neighbour. It is making oneself available to another who is suffering; it is sensitivity to the sufferings of others. So sympathy and compassion alone are not enough. The good Samaritan gave of himself to the other person. The gift was a gift of self.

It is tempting (and often very satisfying) for those of us who give alms to the beggars on our streets, and then go on our way, to feel that we have "done our bit" for the less fortunate among us. Sr

Consilio might well have placed limits on her own generosity - she might well have responded that what she was doing for these "men of the road" was merely in keeping with the ideal of "charitable works". And yet she knew that one cannot give of oneself and remain at a distance from the object of one's attentions. One cannot lend an ear to the troubles and sufferings of others without being touched and transformed in a very real sense. Like the good Samaritan, Sr Consilio would be marked out as one who was "moved" by the misfortunes of others - moved to the point of action, moved to the point of making herself available to those in such great distress.

If the gauge of her love was to be her selflessness, the price of her commitment would be great. In the winter of 1966 she had yet to find the "home" which was so badly needed, or the financial wherewithal to make the dream a reality. With no government support and no wealthy benefactors, the battle would be an uphill one.

The "Dairy" was located across the yard from the convent kitchen. It was used to store milk and butter. Consilio saw the building as a potential location for a kind of "drop-in" centre where she could greet her visitors and listen to their troubles. The young nun would find a way to turn things to her advantage.

"I talked to Sr Patricia about how much more convenient it would be for her to have a fridge rather than trotting back and forth across the yard with the milk and butter. She was in total agreement, which left me with only the bursar, Mother Therese, to convince. The bursar was quite happy to give me the use of the dairy provided it could be replaced by a fridge."

Several days later Sr Consilio came across a second hand fridge advertised for sale in the newspaper. The advertiser lived in Waterford. *"I rang the man who was selling it, telling him how badly I needed it, but that I had no money. I assured him I would pay him for it as soon as I could put £40 together. It seemed a huge sum of money to me at the time. Mother Sacred Heart, Tom* and myself set out*

*Name changed

for Waterford and we took the fridge back to Athy on the roof of Tom's car. In due course the man got his £40..."

The Dairy now became the focal point of Sr Consilio's work with the homeless and the addicts. In addition, another room nearby was made available. By this time, a few tradesmen had begun to recover from their addiction and they set to work on the Dairy and adjoining room. Thus a functioning unit began. Resources were always limited - so much so that there were days when Sr Consilio did not know where the next meal would come from. And there were other problems. Not everyone was supportive of the new development.

The Dairy was situated very close to the school, and while some of the children were fascinated by the men and women they saw coming and going every day, some adults saw these men and women as "undesirables" in the locality.

There were many in the convent who could not understand what was going on, or where it might all end. The numbers of children in the primary and secondary schools were increasing and so too were the numbers of callers to Sr Consilio. Mother Sacred Heart was worried. Reluctantly, she spoke to Consilio about it. *"All is finished now,"* Sr Consilio thought *"what will I do - more important what will all the poor men do?"* Mother Sacred Heart was having sleepless nights and so too was Consilio. The former was anxious to help families and knew that alcohol was the cause of many a family break up. Sr Consilio was experiencing doubts - was it the right place for her at all, was she all wrong? Was she doing what God wanted her to do? She prayed and asked for guidance.

About this time, living near the town of Athy, was a man who was seriously ill from alcoholism. The man said to his mother that Our Lady told him she was to send for Dr Des O'Neill. The mother at first refused - not only was Dr Des not their doctor, but she did not even know of him. However, as the son persisted, and as he was seriously ill she finally relented. When Dr Des saw the man he contacted Sr Consilio and asked her to take him. Knowing how ill he was she was very hesitant, but agreed. That man made a complete recovery and never again took a drink. It was a turning point for Sr Consilio. She had been praying hard to Our Lady and

63

she took this as a sign. If Our Lady saw Cuan Mhuire as fit for her seriously sick son, who was Sr Consilio to doubt? Mother Sacred Heart closed her eyes to Sr Consilio's comings and goings, and her ears to those who doubted - if she hadn't done so there would be no Cuan Mhuire.

In the early days, the Dairy came to be known among some locals as the "Dug-Out", so Sr Consilio felt she must give it a proper name. Her good friend Dr Des O'Neill suggested the name "An Cuan" meaning "The Harbour". Des loved boats and the harbour was the place of shelter for boats when the seas were rough. It seemed the perfect name for this place of refuge. Sr Consilio knew that it would have to include Our Lady's name *as none of this would have been possible without her.*- hence the name "Cuan Mhuire" - "The Harbour of Mary.". In time "Cuan Mhuire" would become synonymous with recovery and re-birth. Indeed it was not long before this new haven was home to thirty men and women, many of them attracted by stories they had heard of the fledgling treatment centre. Thirty people with only the bare necessities - their "bank" a jar on the mantlepiece into which they put whatever spare shillings they had, and from this central fund came the money for the tea, sugar, milk and biscuits that carried them from day to day. Marvellous things were happening within the four walls of the dairy. As the building was reconstructed, people's lives were being built and the fame of Sr Consilio was spreading far and wide. Yet even in these earliest days in the history of Cuan Mhuire, the "seeds" of a programme for recovery were being sown - Sr Consilio held daily "morning meetings" at which household chores were assigned - the cooking, cleaning and general running of the house. Mother Sacred Heart employed some of the residents in the convent garden, thus enabling them to earn a few pounds which they sent to their hard pressed families at home, while they themselves were in recovery.

Cuan Mhuire would be a "treatment centre" with a difference - one modelled on the Christian family where every resident became a member of that family, and where the innate goodness and giftedness of the individual was emphasised. For one thing was crystal clear to Sr Consilio: that those who sought her help were deeply wounded people, who for a multitude of reasons had been brought to their knees and were in need of love and compassion.

At the time confrontational therapy was widely used. Sr Consilio does not believe that there is such a thing as a "hopeless case" where addiction is concerned. And so it has been, from the earliest days of Cuan Mhuire, that Sr Consilio has avoided confrontation, and instead focused on the person's worth and uniqueness as a child of God.

Cuan Mhuire offers a comprehensive, structured, abstinence based, residential programme to persons suffering from alcohol, other chemical dependencies and gambling. While its treatment model draws on the twelve steps of AA, Cuan Mhuire has its own unique programme, developed and perfected over a period of more than thirty years by Sr Consilio and her dedicated team. Total abstinence is the goal of treatment. Since Cuan Mhuire was, and is inspired by the belief that each individual is of eternal value, and that there are no hopeless cases, it's treatment is geared not only towards the individual's addiction, but also towards restoring his/her dignity, self respect and sense of responsibility.

The programme at Cuan Mhuire includes:

- Group Therapy
- One to One Counselling
- Meditation
- Attendance at AA, NA and GA meetings
- Videos, lectures and discussions on all issues associated with addiction and recovery
- Therapeutic duties, which instil a sense of responsibility and help the individual to acquire skills necessary for coping with everyday living when he or she leaves the centre.

While persons of all denominations avail of these services, there is a strong emphasis in Cuan Mhuire on a Spiritual Recovery. The belief is that there is no real recovery without the person's turning his or her will over to the care of God as he, or she, understands Him.

One of Cuan Mhuire's assets is that each centre has a modern, purpose-built detoxification unit, staffed twenty four hours a day by qualified nurses and counsellors. The detoxification programme is carried out under a Medical Director.

Cuan Mhuire also provides a non residential service which incorporates a Two Year After Care Programme for the following:-

- Persons who have satisfactorily completed their treatment programme.
- Relatives of persons who have satisfactorily completed their programme.

These After Care services are provided not only in the various Cuan Mhuire Centres, but at many other locations throughout Ireland.

Sister Consilio never worries unduly about money. Her belief is that Our Lady will look after it. *"The work I do is God's and our Lady's, I am just being allowed give them a hand, that's how I see it"*, she says, *"I feel that when I am gone, Cuan Mhuire will last because it is based on goodness and the desire to help everyone. All you have to do is to be here and see how it happens and you could not but believe that Cuan Mhuire is in the hands of God, and I am very glad to leave things to Him."*

By the early 1970's the Dairy was packed to overflowing with those who were turning up at its doors on a daily basis. It was no longer adequate to house all of those who were in need of a refuge. But where to go? The coffers were empty and it was difficult enough to find the money for the basic necessities, such as food and heating. And yet, Consilio put her faith, as always, in Our Lady. She would not ignore her prayers. Somehow, somewhere, she would establish Cuan Mhuire in its own right, with its own house.

The Dairy: First Cuan Mhuire

Mother Mary of The Sacred Heart

Dr Des O'Neill with his wife Monica and Sr Consilio

Lorcan O'Neill

Cáit O'Neill

Chapter 5

A PLACE TO CALL HOME

"In my Father's house there are many dwelling places. If it were not so, would I have told you that I go to prepare a place for you? And if I go and prepare a place for you, I will come again and will take you to myself, so that where I am, there you may be also."

John 14: 2 - 4

The sign in the estate agent's window advertised the imminent auction of 43 acres of land, just outside Athy. It was November 1972 and the advertisement caught Consilio's eye as she walked through the town one afternoon.

The story of how this nun would come to acquire the land for Cuan Mhuire will be told and re-told for many years to come - as long as there are those who speak for Cuan Mhuire - for as long as Cuan Mhuire is a reality in the lives of others. It is - many would argue - a story of one woman fighting almost insurmountable obstacles, with the odds stacked against her, and yet as the story of Cuan Mhuire unfolds, one is struck by the depth of Consilio's faith in her patron, Our Lady. And one becomes fearful - for those ordinary mortals who think they have the slightest hope of blocking her path, or frustrating her schemes and plans.

On the following Monday morning, Sr Consilio, encouraged by the support of her Mother Superior, paid a visit to the local bank manager. He knew the land she intended to bid for and would later admit that he was hoping another bidder - a local farmer - would get the land in question. Mr Walsh, the bank manager, asked Consilio how she proposed to pay for the land, in the event of her making a successful bid. She told him that "Our Lady" would provide. Sr Consilio attended the auction (in all the nuns regalia, veil and all) accompanied by one of the men from her "Dairy" centre. She came away from the auction with a forty- two acre field and no money to pay for it. After the auction, Mr Walsh, the bank manager, rang the farmer to inquire how he had got on. The farmer replied: "Sure, I hadn't a hope, I hadn't a hope, the little nun got it." Today, Sr Consilio says she cannot recall whether it was herself or her companion who did the actual bidding!

Sr Consilio provides us with her own amusing account of how, the next day, she met with the bank manager and they had a little "chat" about things. *"The day after the auction, Mother Sacred Heart sent me on a message to the bank. The Manager and his assistant were standing inside the counter. He somewhat reluctantly reached his hand over the counter to congratulate me on buying the farm. In the next breath he said 'I want to see you inside', pointing towards his office. I said in response 'I want to see you too, sir'. When we were seated he looked across the desk at me and said 'I stayed awake all night thinking about you, and about what would happen when a big cheque came in and there was nothing to meet it'. 'Well', I said 'I thought about you too last night, but I didn't stay awake all night thinking about you - what I was thinking was that you don't trust me, and that for your sake and for my sake, I will have to find a bank manager, wherever he might be, who will trust me. I have no doubt that there will be many times when Cuan Mhuire will be in the red, but I would not want to get a bank manager into trouble, so I'll just have to find someone who will not worry whether we are 'up' or whether we are 'down'. The bank manager reached out his hand across the desk and said: 'I'm sorry for not trusting you, but I will from now on,' and that is exactly what he did. He trusted, supported and helped me from that day forward."*

Several weeks after this meeting, the vendor of the land died unexpectedly - and in death he provided Sr Consilio and the fledgling Cuan Mhuire with a vital lifeline - time. Sr Consilio had more time to raise the purchase money. Later, Mr Walsh discovered that Sr Consilio had paid off the purchase price in full and he had not to worry about honouring any big cheque. When he asked Consilio how she had managed to pay for the land, she simply replied: *"Our Lady helped me."*

Sr Consilio saw the need even in the earliest days, to provide a firm foundation for her house. This would be no house built on sand. It would come to be rooted in the firm foundations prepared by those friends whom she knew she could trust. This was vital if Cuan Mhuire was to grow and develop for the benefit of future generations - those who were not even born in the first days of Cuan Mhuire - those who have yet to be born even as this book goes to print. The Cuan Mhuire Trust takes the form of a Company Limited by Guarantee to fulfil the requirements of the law. At present it has nine members who appoint three Directors at its Annual General Meeting. Over and above their legal duties acting collectively as a company, the present incumbents also give of their time very generously to help individually in various ways. These are men and women of diverse backgrounds and occupations, from different parts of Ireland. By convention they wish to remain in the background, working quietly and voluntarily. Four are in fact full-time voluntary workers in Cuan Mhuire. Yet, while preferring to remain anonymous themselves, they speak of, and remember with affection and pride, four of the earliest Trustees who have since gone to their heavenly reward:

Seosamh O Cuinneagain was a solicitor, born and reared in Belfast. He set up practice in Enniscorthy, Co. Wexford, where he lived with his wife and children, moving to Dublin in the later years of his life. It was Seosamh who looked after the legal formalities of establishing the Cuan Mhuire Trust, and he acted as secretary of the Trust for several years thereafter. He is fondly remembered as a jovial man. He loved walking long distances in the country - several miles at a time. One learned, later that he was continuously praying; one saw the rosary ring moving on his finger. Seosamh went to his eternal reward on 10th March 1987, after many years of long and loyal service to Cuan Mhuire.

His daughter, Jeanne-Marie Ni Chuinnegain remembers her father as follows: "Seosaimh O Cuinnegain, or simply Joe to those who knew him, was my father. He was a founder Trustee of Cuan Mhuire. Born in Belfast, he taught in Knockbeg College in Carlow and he fought in the Spanish Civil War for Christianity.

Later, he studied Law, married my mother, Bridie Dolan from Galway, and lived on a farm there. Later they moved to Dublin. Shortly afterwards, they moved to Enniscorthy. They had four children, the first three were all born in Galway. After a good pause, I came along, a year after they had moved to Wexford.

My father was very charismatic. People loved him and the few people I know who did not always see eye to eye with him, very much respected him. This was because they saw that my father believed passionately in respect for others. He worked hard to give dignity to people who had lost it.

I have endless memories of my father's goodness. What I admire about him is his generosity and how his greatest acts were kept very private, and I was only aware of some of these when he died. Many people came forward to tell the family about how he had helped them, and I was amazed at the lengths he had gone to on behalf of some people. But I was also aware of many simple kindnesses he performed. While I lived at home, I witnessed such events on a daily basis

He was a very hard-working man. He was a man of vision and he had the courage to see things through against all odds, for the good of the community or of the country. His compassion was boundless, and he stood for justice and dignity for all peoples. He was tolerant and very quick to forgive, but he could be impatient at times about carelessness, abuse, or peoples' sufferings. He had tremendous energy all his life and was disciplined and precise in his duties. I loved his sense of humour and his great story-telling ability. He was a romantic and wrote poetry and prose. He loved my mother so much, and needed her as an anchor. Dad had such vitality, and so many goals to fulfil, that I do not think he could have managed it all if he had not a wife like my mother. She grounded him and complimented his personality so well.

He was in his own words - a Wolfe Tone Republican. My father was very Catholic, deeply religious and very spiritual. Also he was open to other people's beliefs and did not try to enforce his politics or religion on anyone who did no agree with him.

He encouraged tolerance of different Christian religions in Ireland and his desire for a United Ireland was not in order to oppress any denomination, but to get rid of oppression and to give equal opportunity to all people on our island. He was angry at the injustices and prejudices bestowed on minority groups.

To prove this point: he was interned in 1957 for his Republican outspokenness. He was giving unauthorised speeches about injustices and civil rights. He escaped in 1958 and was never caught. A year later the Curragh camp was closed down. But to show how genuine the man was to people, his business became one of the largest local practises in the East and South-East of Ireland, and many of his clients were the Landed Gentry.

That aspect of my father's life fascinated me. That the Landed Gentry could enjoy his company, trust him and promote him as a lawyer, while knowing his deep-rooted Republican ideals.

As a father, my dad was very kind, he was very protective, which was lovely as a child, but became a problem for me in my late teens. He endlessly gave me "protective advise". However, I always knew that it was because he loved me so much.

He did some wonderful unselfish acts for me. For example, it would have suited him very well to have one of his children study law and help him out. My mother encouraged us to do it, but Dad let us "off the hook". As I was the last child - the onus was on me. I had actually commenced Law when my father noticed my distress. He advised me to follow my own heart on what I wanted to do. I knew that was tough for him as he always believed that I would follow in his footsteps. As I changed careers, he encouraged and prized me and I felt that he was genuinely proud of me "as me". It was a very unconditional love.

He had that unconditional respect for people too, even if anybody annoyed him, he forgot it quickly and treated them well.

His close friends were always interesting, a unique kind of people, who were and are, extremely loyal to him. One of these friends is Sr Consilio Fitzgerald. I met her as a child on a few occasions. I was left in no doubt about how much my father revered her. I never heard him so protective or praiseworthy of anyone (outside of family) before. I knew she must be somebody very, very special.

I was so impressed. I would hold her in awe, only she is too modest to want it. She is humble, genuine, full of life, works tirelessly, and believes in peoples' goodness. She has tremendous power of forgiveness and really cares. She is a visionary and has proven what such a gift, combined with courage and tenacity can achieve.

To me, Sr Consilio and my Dad must have really understood each other so well. Two of a kind in my opinion.

As his daughter, I feel his presence so strong. His influence has given me inspiration and courage to go with my intuition in rights and wrongs in life. I thank him for teaching me never to consider myself better than anybody else, and never to look down on anyone. I believe in dignity for all people too. If I hadn't the father that I had, I would have missed out on so much. He was exceptional. But I thank my mother for enabling Dad to do all he did and for her enormous contributions to my life also."

It is a familiar and often repeated story, that those who are possessed of some skill or talent are pressed into service - not out of a sense of duty or obligation to Cuan Mhuire, but out of a love for Consilio and gratitude for the gift of recovery which many found within this sheltered harbour. Of course, she will tell you that Our Lady enlists the help needed at regular intervals and who can refute this claim? The history of Cuan Mhuire's development is inextricably bound up with the life journeys of so many generous and gifted individuals. People who are still so fondly remembered by Sr Consilio, and others whom they touched in so many positive ways.

When Sr Consilio set up her first small residential project beside the convent, it was clear to her that many of those who came seeking shelter were also badly in need of medical attention, their bodies ravaged by years of addiction and neglect. So as Sr Consilio puts it, Our Lady sent her Dr Des O'Neill. Des was then in medical practice in Athy and nearby Ballytore. However, he responded to Cuan Mhuire's needs. Without the help of Dr Des, Sr Consilio would have encountered even more obstacles than she did in getting her treatment centre off the ground. Strange as it may seem, the attitude of the medical establishment in general, at that time - with some honourable exceptions, ranged from indifference to distaste for the addict and addiction.

Faced with the practical problems of putting Cuan Mhuire on a formal business footing, Sr Consilio asked Dr Des to become a trustee of her foundation and in that role and as medical officer to Cuan Mhuire, he remained one of her most valued advisors until his death on February 7th 1990.

Although a modest and self depreciating man with a gentle, amiable manner, Dr Des O'Neill could be extremely tough-minded in defence of his beliefs, the most strongly-held of which were his religion, his nationalism and his dedication to the integrity of Cuan Mhuire.

His early childhood had been spend in Kildare, where his father was a bank manager, and he later came back to school there, in Clongowes Wood, so it was not surprising that he had a great love of racing, especially at the Curragh. In his later years, when he was no longer able to go to the races, he was kept in touch with the racing world through longstanding friends such as Don Dunlea who valued him not only for his worthy qualities, but equally for his ironic sense of humour, which made him the best of company, never earnest, never boring. He is still remembered in Cuan Mhuire with great affection as are his late wife, Monica, and his two beautiful children, Lorcan and Cait.

If Dr Des tended the physical needs of those who passed through Cuan Mhuire, yet another wonderful man was sent to minister to their spiritual needs. For Sr Consilio will reiterate her firm belief that all persons are spiritual beings and that "care of the soul" is vital, on the journey back to life. The "soul doctor'" arrived at Cuan Mhuire in the person of a Dominican priest - Fr Michael Kelly. A former missionary who had worked for years in Trinidad - he would become known as "Cuan Mhuire's Priest". Sr Consilio recalls his arrival at Cuan Mhuire, one freezing November evening in the very early days. He had just returned from Trinidad and had been assigned to work with the Dominicans in Athy. Fr Michael had been in treatment for the "drink problem" some time before his return to Athy, and when next he "broke out" on a binge, the Prior contacted Sr Consilio and asked her to accompany Fr Kelly and himself to the Saint John of God Hospital. He was to spend the next two years in hospital. Sr. Consilio recalls her sadness over his suffering. *"My heart bled for him and I only wished I could have offered him a place to stay, and I hoped and prayed that some day he could return to Athy. From Dublin he was eventually sent to a Dominican House in Montenotte, Cork. Over those few years I visited him whenever I could. He was a great reader; he loved nature; he had a great understanding of life and living. He was a wonderful conversationalist with an unusual sense of humour. Everybody loved Fr Michael."*

Sr Consilio managed to persuade Fr Michael to take up residence in the old dairy. She divided one of the two rooms there to make space for him. She still remembers how easily pleased he was to settle in a room which was cramped and tiny.*"He used to tell me that he had to sit sideways on the toilet as we were in the process of extending the bathroom and bags of cement were in his way!"* In spite of all the inconveniences, Fr Michael settled down and grew to love the place so much.*"He was an extraordinary character, a man of deep faith. We all loved to go to his five o'clock Mass every evening. He never missed the 5 p.m. Mass even when he got old and feeble. He always left his room door open so that anyone who wanted Confession or just a chat was free to walk in."* Fr Michael had a special love for the "men of the road" and they for him. It was characteristic of the man - who continued to keep in touch with his former parishioners in Trinidad many years after he had left that country.

Another Dominican priest who had worked with Fr Michael on the missions told Sr Consilio that Fr Michael was the one priest who had really got through to the people - and when they wanted to emphasise just how much he thought of them they would say "Matt (as he was known to them) has no time for the white man," meaning by this, that he had all the time in the world for them. It took Fr Michael a long time to get sober, after that he gave up cigarettes, but he never forgot or neglected his old friends and for as long as his health permitted him, he went down every morning to the "early house" to meet those who were still caught up in the web of alcoholism. He never gave up on any of them.

He went to bed early, and it was customary for me to go to his room and say some prayers with him after the family Rosary each night. Some nights if I got delayed and didn't turn up he would be very annoyed and come up the corridor saying: "Where is that so and so nun?"

He visited the Dominicans every Sunday for dinner and was invited to return to them, but Fr Michael came to regard Cuan Mhuire as his permanent home. He was more than happy with the care, attention and friendship which he found in Cuan Mhuire. As time went on, and his health was failing, the new Prior suggested that he might like to go to a Nursing Home. Fr Michael said to Sr Consilio "What will I do if I am told to go? I couldn't bear to leave Cuan Mhuire, but I have to do what I am told." Fr Michael became seriously ill in March of 1988. Sr Consilio stayed by his bed holding his hand and praying with him right up until his death on the evening of 11th March. Sr Consilio remembers him with such love and affection: *"He was a man of peace and joy, with a big heart and a beautiful mind. May he rest in peace."*

Fr Michael was the first priest of Cuan Mhuire. Since these early days, many other priests have been a wonderful help to Sr Consilio and members of the Cuan Mhuire family. These were resident priests, priests of the various parishes in which the Cuan Mhuire Centres are established, and others, who down the years were involved in various ways. Cuan Mhuire owes a debt of gratitude to them all.

Eamon (Ned) Nolan was a barrister by profession. His father, Tom Nolan, was a fearless editor of "The Kerryman". Both his father and his uncle, Michael Knightly, were 1916 veterans. Ned inherited a passionate love of justice. He had the courage to stand up and do battle for it, in every aspect of life. He judged on merit and could be relied upon to back the underdog against the exploiter. That made him, from the start, a natural ally of Cuan Mhuire.

He contributed from a unique range of experiences: in his young days, he spent his summers in the Gaeltacht, on the Great Blasket Island. There, living the life of the islanders, as Eamon O' Nuallain, pulling an oar in the naomhog with Pats Tom O'Cearnaigh, their simple and sincere life-style became part of his character. Later, he went to Germany and took its culture into his world-view. He studied Business, Accountancy and Law. His many skills were put generously at the service of the causes he espoused, much to the benefit of those causes.

From his first meeting with Sr Consilio, he became an enthusiastic supporter. He quickly began to enlist his many Kerry friends as co-workers. Constantly travelling between Dublin and Tralee, Ned had the standing and leadership to weld them into an effective support group. Always unassuming, to the point of shyness, when Cuan Mhuire had a task that needed doing, Ned went out and did it.

Sr Consilio tells us that: *"Ned Nolan was one of the finest people I met in my whole life. He was a rare type of friend, who said very little, but thought very deeply. He was one in a million - always loyal and faithful, always working behind the scenes to make Cuan Mhuire a better place. Being a barrister, he understood all the legal aspects of the Trust, and made sure that everything was as it ought to be. His generosity knew no bounds; his home in Kennilworth Square, Dublin, was always 'open house' for all of us, no matter how long we needed it. He was thoughtful and caring. In the early days, I rarely got to bed until the small hours of the morning, and at that stage I would be quite cold. Ned arrived one day with an electric blanket - a rare gift in those times. He wanted to make sure that if I only got a few hours sleep, at least I would be warm.*

He always watched out for me. Having a legal mind, he was quick to see the many pitfalls that I could so easily fall into. If he thought that I wasn't listening to his gentle voice, he sat me down and told me some home truths. He definitely was one of the most honest, decent, generous, caring, committed friends one could ever meet. In a word, he was a man of integrity - one got the impression that he never used surplus words lest they detract from the simple truth to which he was dedicated."

Ned Nolan died on October 4th 1988 after a long and painful battle with lung cancer.

Eddie Walsh is a legend in Cuan Mhuire circles. One gets the impression of a man who was - in so many ways - the epitome of the tormented addict. So full of talent, so gifted and yet so vulnerable and child-like in so many endearing ways. Eddie was one of a Dublin family of builders; he was a carpenter by trade. He was one of the founding members of Cuan Mhuire. In his youth,

Eddie had emigrated to England, and from there to Canada, settling eventually in Alaska. Deeply in trouble with alcoholism, Eddie's family brought him home to Dublin and sought Sr Consilio's help. She met Eddie and his brother at Dublin Airport . She took him to the original Cuan Mhuire. He was in very bad shape. Sr Consilio recalls the circumstances of their first meeting. *"I will always remember collecting Eddie about 2 am off a plane in Dublin Airport. He had had a long trip with quite a few stops from Alaska. He had his pockets filled with all the miniatures of drink he had bought on the plane, as he knew that the pubs would all be closed when he arrived in Ireland. He also knew that because of his addiction he had to get some alcohol into his system before morning. Little did I realise that it was the first of many journeys I would make with him around the country and back to Dublin."*

Eddie proved to be a real "Godsend" at the time that the first Cuan Mhuire was being built. Help was scarce and there was no money. Whatever money Eddie brought home with him, he spent on building materials. "Eddie Alaska", as he came to be known (and by which name he is fondly remembered) was a generous and caring person who had suffered enormously in life and who continued to suffer until his untimely death twenty years later.

Sr Consilio recalls: *"When I first met Eddie I had very little insight into the enormity of the fears, the guilt, the remorse and the self hatred that haunts the lives of people who suffer from addiction. I have no doubt but that Eddie was sent to be my teacher as he was the epitome of all the above. Even though I did the best I could to help him along the way I regret that I didn't understand better the terrible anguish he suffered. Looking back now, I know there were times when I had expectations of him and felt he could do more about getting sober. Today, with the insights I have gained, I realise I was only adding to his already heavy load. Had I these insights earlier I might well have approached the situation differently."*

Eddie, as a child, had experienced having to make do with little, and his ability to make a little go a long way was not lost on Cuan Mhuire. He accompanied Sr Consilio to many auctions to buy second hand materials. Sr Consilio's account of those early efforts is as follows: *"Eddie knew Dublin like the back of his hand. A friend*

(Phil*) from Galway had given us a mini van so we went in and out of lane ways in our mini, collecting and buying bits and pieces to put our house together. Years later when we opened our house in Bruree and much later in Newry, Eddie was by my side guiding and helping me all the way. His care for other people knew no bounds. His bed he readily gave to anybody who needed it. I saw him wash people's feet when they were bruised and sore from travelling. He stayed up night after night with those who were disturbed in any way."

On one such occasion, there was a man in the house called Bob Furlong*. He was mentally very disturbed. Some other residents told Sr Consilio that for as long as he stayed in the house they would be afraid to sleep at night. Bob had no place to go so Sr Consilio decided to stay with him herself to allay the fears of the other members of the family. *"About 1 am as we sat in the room, Eddie and Bob talked non-stop. I closed my eyes as I hadn't had any sleep for the previous two nights. After a while the conversation grew quieter and quieter. They thought I was falling asleep and Eddie suggested that Bob and himself go up to the kitchen. Bob, who was supposed to be completely deranged, switched off the light. Then I heard him saying out loud as he left the room: 'I'd better take care of Sister in case some maniac comes the way'..."*

Eddie Alaska seemed to have a "sixth sense" when it came to people being ill or in danger. He was always on the alert for any difficulties that might arise. *"His whole life and concern was for Cuan Mhuire and its people, which he loved so dearly. To this very time a day seldom passes in Cuan Mhuire that Eddie's name is not mentioned with love and affection. He is remembered by thousands of people whose burdens he lightened in so many different ways. Eddie was a very gentle, principled, caring and considerate person. He endured the ongoing terrible pain of the fearful, anxious child within. The idealist who was frustrated by not being able to reach the too-high standards he set for himself - the goodness within him which others saw but he could not see because of his poor self-image."* It is a measure of the profound impression which this man made on Sr Consilio that when you get her on the topic of Eddie she has story after story to recount about this wonderful individual:*"On one occasion he had taken a few drinks,*

* Names changed

82

and as usual the guilt haunted him. He slept across the corridor from Fr Michael (Kelly), so he decided to go to Confession. Having told all the sins he could remember he got absolution. When he got back to his room he remembered something he had forgotten to tell. He went back to Fr Michael who then forgave him for all the sins he had confessed. Once again, Eddie had only got back to his room when he remembered something else he wanted to confess, so he returned a third time to Fr Michael. Fr Michael seeing him for the third time in almost as many minutes let out a roar at him 'Eddie I forgave you, God forgave you, now will you so-and-so off and forgive yourself'.'

He was a loyal and faithful friend. He had great devotion to the Little Flower - Saint Therese, and to Our Lady. He always asked Sister Helen to sing, after the Consecration, 'Jesus Remember Me when you come into Your Kingdom'.- The words of the repentant thief on Calvary. As he lay on the road after being hit by a lorry, two priests coming from different directions whispered the words of absolution in his ear - while I am confident the Lord Himself said at the same time: 'This day you will be with me in Paradise.' May he Rest in Peace. I loved Eddie dearly, I miss him badly, but I feel strongly that he is near and that he is doing for me from Heaven what he tried to do on earth. To me he was an Anam Cara - a soul friend". Eddie died on 26th October 1991. His mortal remains lie in the Cuan Mhuire plot in Athy Cemetery.

"My first introduction to Bishop Kavanagh came through Fr Pollock OP When the Cuan Mhuire Trust was initially set up, Cuan Mhuire owned literally nothing. Later, when the farm was bought and the new Cuan Mhuire built, it became obvious that things had to be formalised - we needed two more trustees. Consequently, a meeting was called and those whom it was felt would be most suited were invited to attend. After the meeting commenced I felt a deep down uneasiness. I told the others how I felt and somebody suggested that we say the Memorare. Just then there was a knock on the door. Fr Pollock OP. wanted to see me. When I told him what was happening he advised me to go no further that day and to go and see Bishop Kavanagh. Fr Pollock arranged a meeting for later on that week.
I remember so well our first meeting. His housekeeper May, whom I later got to know very well, had a beautiful meal prepared for us. Bishop Kavanagh gave us a warm welcome and listened to all the ins and outs of Cuan Mhuire. He was so pleasant and homely I felt at ease straight away. I felt that I had found the friend I needed most at that

time and for many years to come, right down to this present day. Nowhere on earth could you find the likes of Bishop Kavanagh. I know for sure that without his support, his guidance, his trust especially at a time when I doubted myself, Cuan Mhuire would not have been able to continue. The obstacles at that time from within and without were too great. My superiors were too fearful and couldn't understand what Cuan Mhuire was all about. Undoubtedly, they dreaded, and understandably so, what I could walk myself and the Congregation into.

Bishop Kavanagh has opened and blessed all our houses and for many years he came to Galilee House of Studies to confer the Diploma in Counselling on our Graduates. Whenever he visits, it is like a breath of fresh air. He is a man of faith, prayer, and discernment. He has great devotion to Our Lady. She surely sent him to be our guide and counsellor.

He is someone who will never grow old. He loves to smoke his pipe and enjoy a game of golf. His smile is always re-assuring. How blessed are we to know him as our friend. His contribution to Cuan Mhuire will only be known in the life to come."

When Sr Consilio started in Athy, Dr Bertie Blake was the RMS, in Carlow Psychiatric Hospital. He was quick to see the value of Sr Consilio's work and to support her in every way possible. He visited the new Cuan Mhuire on a very regular basis. He not only treated any of her residents who were in need of psychiatric treatment, but he constantly sent patients to her.
He was a tremendous support - always ready and willing to help her. Sr Consilio remembers Dr Bertie with deep gratitude as one of her best friends in those early, difficult days. May he have his eternal reward.

Chris Delaney was the visiting psychiatric nurse. He was most faithful to his weekly visit to the Cuan where he was always available to those who needed a listening ear. Later, he worked in Cuan Mhuire for a number of years. Sr Consilio feels that his contribution could never be measured and that Cuan Mhuire will be forever grateful to him.

One could not write about Cuan Mhuire without writing about that big hearted, far seeing nun - Mother Mary of the Sacred Heart. Sr

Consilio is always quick to point out that were it not for her trusting superior, Cuan Mhuire could never have happened.

Bridie Blanchfield (Mother Mary of the Sacred Heart) - a farmer's daughter, was born on January 31st 1910. She was educated at the Loreto Convent and entered the Convent of Mercy in Athy. She trained as a primary school teacher in Carysfort College and returned to teach in the Athy convent primary school until her appointment as superior of that convent.

She gave great support to all works of mercy and was ever ready to help the needy and deprived. However, her very special interest was Cuan Mhuire and Sr Consilio's work for alcoholics. During difficult, turbulent times, Sr Consilio knew that she had the total backing of her superior - a support without which she couldn't have started, never mind persevered in the work. What other superior of the sixties would have allowed one of her most junior nuns to bid £49,000 for a farm of land knowing in her heart that the nun hadn't a penny to meet the purchase price? What other superior would have such faith and trust?

She lived to see the fruits of that trust, in the thousands of people she saw being helped by Cuan Mhuire, in the four provinces of Ireland. She was a truly great woman who was destined to play a role in the recovery of many.

Sr Consilio now had her bit of land in Athy. The Dairy was filled to overflowing with her "family" - a real building was needed - a place they could really call "home". But how would she manage it? Even should she get the necessary funds together to make the start, Sr Consilio knew that she would need to engage an architect if the building was to be built along pre-planned lines. An architect costs money - money Sr Consilio hadn't got. She recalls how she prayed her favourite prayer over and over again. - the Memorare *"Remember O most gracious Virgin Mary that never was it known that anyone who fled to your protection was left unaided".* Then the next miracle happened.

One day, Sr Consilio looked out the window and saw a man staggering up the avenue. He had a distinguished look about him; he was well dressed with greying hair and he had a handsomely lined face. Sr Consilio recalls thinking, as she watched him approach - *"Could this be the architect I am looking for"?* The man's name was Bob Gibson from Banbridge in County Down, and he was indeed the architect she had been praying for - Our Lady had not let her down! Bob was a kindly and enthusiastic man, who, on recovering, took complete charge of the planning of Sr Consilio's first major Cuan Mhuire building project.

The task would be a daunting one. It would have defeated the toughest, most resilient of people. However, once again, the "little nun" from Athy showed her mettle and her unrivalled capacity for optimism and faith in the face of the toughest of obstacles.*"This was the hardest time,"* Sr Consilio says, looking back. There were days when few turned up for work but in spite of the "stop-start" nature of the work, things got done, and the building was completed. There were days, too, when the "little nun" put others to shame as she shouldered her share of the manual labour. Once more, Sr Consilio enlisted Our Lady's help and once more she came to the aid of Cuan Mhuire.

The story is told, by one of those who worked on the building, of how the bill for wooden trusses got paid. *"I'll always remember the trusses because I was working on the site at the time. They cost £900. F.T. Buckley, Builders Providers, Dublin, had given Sr Consilio two years credit for materials but the trusses came from Cork, and had to be paid for 'cash on delivery'. I remember they were due to be delivered on the Thursday of a week when there was no money available. On the Tuesday morning Sr Consilio came out to us waving a cheque for £1,000. 'Look' she said , 'Our Lady has sent us the money two days too soon'! Our Lady hadn't in fact miscalculated the day - a few hours later the lorry arrived from Cork with the trusses - the consignment was mistakenly sent two days early! I'll never forget her face when she saw the trusses on the lorry. 'Our Lady knew, even though we didn't, and she sent the money on time - she always knows'."*

One of Cuan Mhuire's most precious possessions is a picture of Our Lady of Perpetual Succour. In August 1980 a fire broke out in a wing of the treatment centre. One room was completely and utterly destroyed. To the amazement of all, this particular picture was found intact amid the smouldering rubble. No doubt Our Lady was giving a message - a message that wasn't lost on Sr·

Consilio and the residents as they stood in the courtyard and recited the Memorare.

The task of running the new building was no less formidable than that of the reconstruction - feeding, housing and often clothing many of the residents. And yet Our Lady sent Sr Consilio all the right people as and when, they were needed. Des O'Neill, Ned Nolan, Fr Michael, Bob Gibson and Eddie Walsh - all of whom gave of themselves and their abundant talents selflessly in those early days. These were joined by farmers, nurses, builders, chefs, electricians, plumbers and so many others who had come to Cuan Mhuire looking for help and found that they could give something in return to Cuan Mhuire. This was a "community" in the true sense of the word - where people worked, prayed, shared and recovered together.

Sr Consilio's father summed it up when he wrote the following poem in the mid1960's:

The Harbour

There is a place called Cardington,
Adjacent to Athy,
Where some gentle folk assemble,
In an effort to keep dry.
Mostly all have been successful -
There are few who have their breaks
There are many good and upright men
Who once were roving rakes.

Now, how this good thing started,
I barely have a clue.
The decent neighbours gave a hand,
And the nuns must get their due.
It was they who kept things moving
Although busy in their schools.
And I'd nearly say in doing their part
They had to stretch the rules.

Men gathered here from many parts,
And every walk of life;
Some that never married,
And some that chanced a wife.
Architects and engineers
And willing working men;
And some I'm sure who sold their shirts
In hopes to keep their skin.

And the girls came, and what a change,
Since they wore a dress and bib.
Some blame Jimmy Hennessy,
More think 'tis "women's lib".
'Tis right to help the ladies
Things are no good done by halves,
And I would have come sooner
But I could not sell the calves.

They are going to build a modest home,
To shelter those in need;
No word about your past life,
Or no word about your creed,
You are welcome to "The Harbour"
Where Our Lady gives the beck
To the barely out of order,
Or the hopeless looking wreck.

This country is improving,
Growing tomatoes in the bogs,
And somewhere up near Dublin
There's a cat's home for the dogs
The cows are milked in parlours
The pigs are all hygiene
And don't you think 'tis high time
To help the human being.

Maurice Fitzgerald

Those early days had their bright moments and embarrassing incidents too. One such incident occurred when Sr Consilio was invited by a Health Authority to sit on a selection board to make new appointments in the field of alcoholism treatment.

Sr Consilio recalls the events of that day: *"The occasion demanded that I should be smart and formal. In those times, for a nun, a spotless black habit, and starched white cap was the order of the day. I had only one habit, made by myself, and no longer pristine. Accordingly, the cap was in the wash, and the habit rolled up ready to be cleaned, on the day before the session I was due to attend.*

At noon, the phone rang. The interviews were already in progress in the boardroom. What was the delay? My presence was expected at once I had mistaken the day. Panic...

Putting on the wet cap, and the crumpled habit, I waylaid a priest friend, and his companion, who were just off on a fishing trip. To their inconvenience, but evident amusement, we set off at speed in their car for the mental hospital some miles away. Worse was to come. On the way, it became evident that not only was my habit rather dishevelled, it was actually falling apart. My slip was going to be showing, literally as well as metaphorically.

High speed emergency repairs were carried out with the aid of a fishing line and the skill and inventiveness of the anglers. Speed limits were flouted, and in record time we were at the hospital.

I arrived breathless, dodged surprised-looking orderlies, and took my place in the boardroom - a most unusual looking nun, amongst a bemused panel of psychology experts. Steam still arose from my freshly washed, still wet cap, giving a whole new meaning to the notion of a 'drying-out unit'! Assorted salmon flies were attached to my black habit, precariously holding together it's disintegrating parts. What the senior psychiatrist made of it, history does not record. Perhaps, for him it was all in a day's work.

What I do remember is that by the end of the afternoon, the most suitable candidates had been appointed. As so often, in my experience, the objective was achieved, if in circumstances quite other than I had planned. Usually, it is with the best will in the world, that we inadvertently lay these 'banana skins' for ourselves.

On another occasion the local Bishop came to visit a Cuan Mhuire house that was only recently up and running. To get everything shipshape, we had stored away all the clutter in my bedroom. After being shown all around, the Bishop expressed himself delighted with the set-up. What inspired him, I wondered afterwards, to add: 'I seem to have seen everywhere, except your own living quarters'. The door of my room was pushed open with difficulty. It revealed - to his bewilderment, and my chagrin, - piled high to the ceiling, every object imaginable -it was apparently the dwelling place of a kleptomaniac."

More recently, at another of the Cuan Mhuire houses, they had some distinguished guests coming to join them for a meal. Just beforehand, Sister met a black suited stranger in the hallway, looking lost. She helpfully suggested to him that *"perhaps he had come to the wrong place, maybe he had an appointment elsewhere in the neighbourhood"*, - then it suddenly dawned on her that he was the Bishop and she herself had indeed invited him to come. That day she had completely forgotten about it. Despite this minor hiccup, the lunch party was enjoyed by all concerned, including the Bishop.

Such moments are certainly most deflating, but when all is said and done, they simply show us that we are human. The discomfort quickly fades, leaving only pleasurable memories of fate's comic interludes. On balance, Sr Consilio says: *"I am glad of them all, and I hope that other people who have been embroiled in moments of my aberration have gained from them amusement, insights and on occasion, perhaps even a free lunch - but never any lasting hurt."*

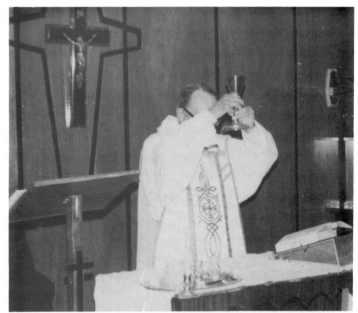

Fr Michael Kelly

Eddie Walsh

Bishop Kavanagh and Sr Consilio

Ned Nolan

Seosamh Cuinneagain

Dr Bertie Blake

*Sr Consilio and Bob Gibson
in Lourdes*

*Cuan Mhuire's first new car
Presented by Michael O'Reilly of Windsor Motors*

95

Chapter 6

ANOTHER PLACE TO CALL HOME

*"I will go before you and I will
Humble the great ones of the earth:
I will break in pieces the gates of brass
And I will burst the bars of iron
And I will give hidden treasures
And the concealed riches of secret places:
That you may know that
I am the Lord
The God of Israel who calls
You by your name."*

Isaiah 45: 2-3

An Indian Guru once advised a disciple who asked him how best he might approach the well-charted, but often stormy seas of life. "Be realistic - plan for miracles".

We rise from our beds in the morning; we live lives so blessed and renewed by the challenges which confront us, often in the guise of great personal difficulties, seemingly insurmountable problems, difficult, or worse, indifferent people - and in meeting these challenges we are part of, and witness to, a never-ending succession of miracles.

And how our lives can unfold and surprise us! The young nun finds that, sooner than she might have expected, the house is not nearly big enough to accommodate and provide sanctuary for the afflicted. As hundreds of men and women pack Athy House and the surrounding portakabins to overflowing - more miracles are needed. Athy is a long way from Kerry, Cork, or Limerick - a bridge too far for many of the desperate men and women of Munster, and yet a glance at the admissions book will show that a large percentage of the Athy House's residents are natives of the Munster area. It is clear - by the mid 70's - that more must be done; there are other and more daunting mountains to climb. But where to obtain the necessary finances with which to acquire a house in the southernmost reaches of the country? Of course, by this time, those close friends and loyal assistants have grown quite accustomed to miracles - both on their own personal journeys and in the unfolding story of Cuan Mhuire.

They will tell you of Sr Consilio's infectious enthusiasm, of how single-minded this woman can be when she has set her mind to the immediate task before her. Problems do not confront Sr Consilio - it is she who confronts the problems. And before you know it - she has the problems "on the run". And what is this tenacity of approach but singular proof - if proof were needed - that these "problems" are God's way of demonstrating to those who have eyes to see and proclaiming to those who have ears to hear, that if Our Lady is with us, who can be against us? *"If Our Lady needs this place for Her work, then we will get it."*

So saying, she tied a Green Scapular around the branch of a tree which overhung the boundary wall of Bruree House, in Bruree, Co Limerick, which had come on the market in early 1977 and which would become the second Cuan Mhuire. She had arrived (without an appointment) to view the property and found the gates locked. Another miracle, another milestone in the story of Cuan Mhuire - another large bank loan to repay.

Bruree House was a famous stud farm. It was home to Galteemore, - the first Irish bred, Irish owned colt to win the Derby. In 1900 Galteemore's half brother, Ardpatrick grew to maturity on the Bruree paddocks. He too lived up to his promise by winning the Epsom Derby. In more recent times when Bruree House was owned by Lady Ursula Vernon, daughter of the Duke of Westminster, its stud farm was again famous - this time because of the racehorse Arkle who was owned by Anne - the last of the Duke's many wives.

October 10th 1977 sees the arrival of the first three men from Athy, to take up residence in Bruree House - Willie Baggott, John Somerville and John Power. Late in the evening of the first day John Somerville and John Power would set out for Rockchapel to the home of Johnny Fitzgerald. They returned the following day with a tractor and trailer which Johnny had given Cuan Mhuire to help "get the place started". Willie would spend the first night alone in this House, except for the company of a friendly dog which appeared as if he "came with the place".

These early days saw many colourful characters in Cuan Mhuire, Bruree - notably Marie Antoinette O'Neill, and Captain Jim Cullen. Tony, as she was better known, would say herself that she "arrived by chance and stayed by choice." She will long be remembered for her graciousness and courtesy. The Captain was of Second World War fame. He saw Cuan Mhuire as his ship and took pride in helping to steer it. Both Tony, and the Captain are gone to their heavenly reward. Tony is buried in the Cuan Mhuire plot in Garrrouse Cemetery, Bruree. Then, there was Dan Walsh who erected the stations of the cross on the perimeter of the walled garden. He commented as he finished the work "maybe on Good Friday somebody will make these stations." This comment was remembered a few weeks later when Dan met an untimely death, and was laid to rest in a quiet County Cork graveyard on Good Friday.

February 1978 saw the arrival of John Moynihan (also from Cuan Mhuire, Athy). Such was the constant and pressing need for money to service the loans, and to maintain and run the new House, that he would spend long hours on the road fund-raising. That did not deter him from playing an active part in the internal affairs of the house. Young and old looked forward to his meetings. To the newcomer he became a friend and guide; to the long stay resident he was a brother to be looked up to; to all he was an example of commitment and dedication to Cuan Mhuire.

How many of us look back over life's journey - to the ostensibly "chaotic" and "random" events in our lives - and fail to see the intricate tapestry that was being woven all along the way? How to make God laugh? Tell him all your plans. For as sure as the traveller sets out for a destination in the East, he will find himself in the West - as high as the ambitious man has set his sights, so he too will be brought low, and where he set out in search of gold - he will become a potter and fashion something of value from the tools and materials provided him. Like the gold for which he has such avarice, he is ultimately tested in the furnace and not found wanting.

And so they continued to find Cuan Mhuire or Cuan Mhuire found them - those in need of help, love and sanctuary. Many would come to a deeper understanding of their uniqueness as men and women made in the image and likeness of a loving God.

There were others who would arrive at Cuan Mhuire by a confluence of circumstances which would, in Sr Consilio's mind, reinforce her belief that Our Lady was guiding their every step as though there was a certain inevitability about their journey.

One such individual was Nurse Jim Donnan who came to Cuan Mhuire, Athy, "to do a few weeks night duty while I was waiting to take up another post" - that was well over twenty years ago! Sr Consilio says of Jim: *"He struck me as being very sound, solid and well rooted. He has a wide range of experience in the nursing field as well as having spent some years as a nurses' tutor. He seemed capable, confident, and well able to get on with the business of taking care of people. At the time, to put it mildly, I was very short staffed and I had a lot on my plate. I surely appreciated having my new helper. At that time there were about one hundred residents from all walks of life at different stages of recovery - many were quite ill and others psychologically disturbed. In those early days Jim and I had little time for long conversations, but I saw very clearly that he was getting on with his work and doing a good job. The weeks passed by, and to my delight, he never mentioned moving on. Perhaps without knowing it, that may have been another reason why I didn't spend time chatting with him in case he mentioned leaving, as he was so badly needed. "*

About three months after he had first arrived at the Athy House, Jim went early one morning to see Sr Consilio. He recalls how, when he started on night duty she had simply told him: *"Jim, just do the best you can, but don't be worrying because Our Lady looks after us"*. He had taken this with a "pinch of salt"; yet now he had come to the conviction that Our Lady was looking after Cuan Mhuire and all of its inhabitants. "I can honestly say that I have worked in many institutions where all kinds of precautions were taken; there were all kinds of staff, and in spite of that, tragedies happened. I can tell you now that I am more convinced than ever, that there is somebody up there looking after us. If there wasn't, this place would not be possible."

Jim Donnan was to stay on with Sr Consilio and Cuan Mhuire, moving from Athy to Bruree House in 1978. Sr Consilio will leave no one in doubt as to the qualities which he has brought to Cuan Mhuire and to all those with whom he comes into contact. *"His love, his loyalty, and his dedication to Cuan Mhuire, to Sr Agnes and myself could never be measured. All these years he worked tirelessly for the betterment of everyone. His counselling skills, his deep understanding of human nature, his love for young and old has equipped him to do a unique job. He is not satisfied with doing his ordinary work, he has also spent long hours on collections in order to keep the dinner on the table.*

Jim could be described as 'The Marathon Man of Cuan Mhuire'. Over the past seventeen years he has taken part in the Dublin City Marathon with all the proceeds from the sponsored run going directly to Cuan Mhuire. When I met him as he had finished the race two years ago I just burst into tears when I saw the state of him, his legs all swollen and sore. This year I pleaded with him not to do it but he was determined. He wanted to collect the much needed money. I am glad that I did not meet him afterwards because from what I am told he was shattered after the twenty six mile run. People like Jim are few and far between - to meet one in a lifetime is a real gift."

When Cuan Mhuire initiated an "Outreach Programme" for schools, youth groups and parents, Jim Donnan was to the forefront. He saw the need to give young people and their parents the message regarding addiction, and he spared neither time nor effort in carrying the message. Today, Jim is on the faculty of Galilee House of Studies where he lectures on addiction to the students doing the Two Year Diploma Course in Counselling.

And the miracles continued. It would not be long before Cuan Mhuire Bruree, as had been the case with Athy, was filled to overflowing with people seeking help. The main house, built in the 1880's was a fine example of a solidly constructed country gentleman's residence. This section of the building had been well maintained. However, many other parts of the building required extensive renovation, if they were to be rendered fit for human habitation. The grain lofts and stables, and the upstairs quarters in the old courtyard, which had been used to accommodate stable hands, were no longer habitable.

It is a mark of the powerful rehabilitative effect which the Cuan Mhuire programme has on the people who pass through its doors that they rediscovered - or sometimes discovered for the very first time - gifts and talents for everything from block laying to carpentry, to plumbing, to gardening or to farming. Cuan Mhuire is more important than the buildings which house those for whom it is a haven, and yet these buildings, with their superb workmanship and their gardens and nurseries, are monuments to the achievements of the thousands of men and women rescued from the oblivion into which they had sunk.

And so it was that the early residents of Cuan Mhuire Bruree, with chisels and sledgehammers, and fortified by a new-found faith in themselves, set about the task of rebuilding and restoring the many grain lofts and stables.

On February 11th 1983 - The Feast of Our Lady of Lourdes - a twenty five bed detoxification unit was ready for occupation. However, it was not until August 8th 1994 that the major reconstruction work on sleeping accommodation and communal facilities took off.

Johnny Fitzgerald, Sr Consilio's brother, a builder by trade, would come to her aid. Every day during the course of reconstruction work, he travelled a return journey of ninety miles to supervise, plan, and work on the building. The work of reconstruction was almost entirely the work of people who had recovered in one or other of the Cuan Mhuire houses. These were gifted, talented men, who wanted to do something to help their fellow sufferers and who consequently, counted neither time nor effort.

Today, the old pre-famine building with its imposing clock tower has been completely restored and reconstructed. It retains the character which was, and is, its distinctive hallmark. The architectural integrity has been preserved - it is in line with the perfection that is the hallmark of all that John Fitzgerald does. Undoubtedly, he is a man with a remarkable attention to detail.

There is now accommodation at Cuan Mhuire, Bruree for one hundred and twenty people. There is a fine games room, coffee bar, assembly hall and a number of therapy rooms. More than seven hundred people attended the official opening of the reconstructed building on Saturday May 18th 1996. Sr Consilio's staunch friend, Bishop James Kavanagh, officiated on the occasion of the opening.

He spoke eloquently during the open air Mass: "The Glory of Cuan Mhuire is that men and women are welcome here from all walks of life. Here, they meet - above all - love, a love that flows from the Hearts of Christ and Our Lady. Each person begins to understand that he or she is a person of immense dignity and worth. Sr Consilio, Sr Agnes and all their wonderful helpers bring Christ's love and respect to every resident in Cuan Mhuire, and the residents themselves respond with loving care to those around them."

The ceremony was also attended by the newly installed Bishop of Limerick, Donal Murray DD, by Canon Greene, Parish Priest of Bruree, Fr J Keating CC Bruree, Fr Dominic O'Neill OP and many visiting clergy.

The following is a letter from Sr Consilio to the family in Cuan Mhuire, Bruree, after the opening of the reconstructed building.

Dear Sister Agnes, Nurses and Family Members,

Now that I am back in Galway and have time to breathe again, I want to say to all of you how amazed I am, and how delighted I am to see Bruree looking so beautiful and in such good shape. It is a real credit, and an example of what can be achieved when people like yourselves get together. I witnessed on my many visits, the hard work put into making the place what it is today. The great team work and spirit that motivated so many to be so committed and dedicated shows the pride you have in Cuan Mhuire. It definitely was unconditional love at its best. The day of the opening was surely a day to be remembered by all who were there. So many have commented on the wonder of it all - far too many to mention. Everything went so well and was so well organised that there didn't seem to be a single hitch.

What has happened to the house is no doubt only a glimmer of what is happening in your lives. I remember that for many who worked on the new building in Athy, it was a real turning point in their lives. The commitment and hard work you practised so well over the past number of months in Bruree, you will be able to continue when you leave, and in this way you will discover more of your giftedness and goodness in the years ahead.

All I can say now is, that I sincerely hope you will all enjoy your new surroundings, and care for them so that they will be just as beautiful for all others who come for help. Again I want to say thanks to all of you; you are an example to all other Cuan Mhuire Houses in so many ways. I also want to say how much I appreciate all the help you have given us in Gardiner Street and here in Galway.

May God and His Blessed Mother always guard you.

Love from,

Sister Consilio.

The final stage of reconstruction at Bruree House - the fourth side of the impressive courtyard, was undertaken in 1997. Once again, Johnny Fitzgerald took charge of the project and this time added sleeping accommodation and extra facilities for a further thirty four persons. The architect of the entire project was Mr Pat Magee of County Down. He travelled from one end of the country to the other to be part of the team.

The spirit and organisation of this second Cuan Mhuire follows the same lines as the original Cuan Mhuire in Athy. As in Athy, the great majority of those who come to Bruree for help are dependent on alcohol, or in a minority of cases, other drugs or gambling. They are at various stages of the progression of addiction, and their direction or purpose in life has often been lost or dimmed. All are in some degree of "hopelessness", some feel rejected by family members and friends; several have lapsed from the practise of their religion, and many have found themselves in a state of continuous inner conflict.

Firstly, they are helped to recover physically. The detoxification procedure under the direction of a doctor, follows the pattern used generally in hospitals and alcoholic units. They are then helped to recognise the nature of their problem. This is facilitated by group therapy, one-to-one counselling, lectures, dissemination of information through audio and video tapes etc. Emphasis is placed on a spiritual solution; faith and hope are restored by a renewed vision of the purpose in life for which each of us was created. The experience of being accepted, cared for, loved and of being able to reciprocate, is central to the spirit of Cuan Mhuire.

Cuan Mhuire is modelled on the Christian Family. The objective is for each person to change himself or herself by involvement in, sharing with, and caring for all the other members of the family. The emphasis is on one community - one family. Every effort is made to help with personal and family problems, and where possible, to restore people to the centre of their own families.

All centres are staffed twenty four hours a day by qualified Nurses and Counsellors. Each person is encouraged to take responsibility for his or her own life. As the person becomes physically well, he or she is expected to take responsibility for some task in the house.

At first, these therapeutic duties may only involve taking responsibility for making one's own bed, or for keeping one's room clean and tidy. There is always a wide cross section of skills and trades represented in the group, thus many unskilled people, especially the young, of whom there are more and more now seeking help, have an opportunity to learn a skill or craft while in rehabilitation. Some volunteer to help in the kitchen, where they aspire to learn basic skills which will help them later to cope with life in a flat or a bedsit.

Back in the days of the earliest Cuan Mhuire - the old dairy beside the convent - people had been coming from the North of Ireland seeking help. Indeed, as mentioned earlier, when Cuan Mhuire moved from the convent site, it was an architect from Banbridge, County Down, then a resident, who designed what was then "the new building". The Northern counties had been generous with financial contributions down through the years. It was fitting then, that when many people were calling for a Cuan Mhuire in the North these calls should be positively responded to. Over a period of time many sites were considered.

Then in early 1983 Fr Rice, who was a prominent member of the Pioneer Total Abstinence Association, informed Sr Consilio that the Good Shepherd Convent near Newry, County Down in the Armagh Diocese, was becoming available, as the Good Shepherd Order were closing that particular convent. Sr Consilio accompanied by some of her colleagues and trustees of Cuan Mhuire, went to Newry to visit and see the convent. The Good Shepherd Sisters, and some women who had stayed with them over the years were still in residence. The visitors were struck by the tangible atmosphere of love within the convent. It was as if all the years of prayer and sacrifice had permeated the building. Structurally the building was suitable, so a decision to go ahead and acquire the convent was made. Cardinal Tomas O'Fiaich, then Archbishop of Armagh gave the project his blessing and was most kind and helpful. Members of the local community were generous with their help.

Sr Consilio writes of Cardinal O'Fiaich: *"When it was suggested to us to purchase the Good Shepherd Convent in Newry, and to open a Cuan Mhuire house there, I went to visit the Cardinal. After he welcomed me* in his own homely fashion, and his housekeeper brought in tea and homemade scones, I told him what we were hoping to do. He said 'if there are nine or ten nuns there at present and they cannot continue to run the place how can you propose to do it on your own?' Well I said; I would not dream of attempting to run it if I were on my own, but I know Our Lady will be there to help me, 'In that case' he said, 'you will be alright'.

Like Bishop Kavanagh, and no doubt he was in touch with Bishop Kavanagh, I found him to be a tower of strength. He visited us on many occasions. His visits were always uplifting. He was the sort of man who made you feel safe and secure. His positive outlook on life, his words of encouragement, meant so much in those early days. When it appeared I was on my last legs, having to make a choice between Cuan Mhuire and the Sisters of Mercy, he went to Rome to find out what steps I would need to take if I found myself on my own. He told my Mother General that I would be welcome in his Diocese, and that he saw Cuan Mhuire as having an important role to play in Religious Life in time to come. Fortunately for me, I didn't have to make the choice in the end. I am glad to be a Sister of Mercy in my own far out way - following as best I can in the footsteps of Mother McCauley - the Foundress of the Sisters of Mercy.

At that time the Cardinal appointed Monsignor Bradley as Parish Priest of Bessbrook (the parish we belonged to), to be a guide and helper for us - a task he has performed magnificently ever since. He looks after our Cuan Mhuire family in a very special way.

Many years earlier, the Cardinal gave my sister, Sr Agnes, his full support when she was anxious to come and help me in Cuan Mhuire - as the following letter testifies:

Ara Coeli
Ard Mhach/Armagh

21st April, 1982

Dear Sister M. Agnes,

I am very happy to approve of your proposal to join your sister in her work for alcoholics at the new centre which has just been opened in Bruree, County Limerick.

It is very necessary work and one which is becoming even more urgent in recent years because of the increase in drinking among young people.

It will also bring you near your beloved Abbeyfeale for which I have a soft spot since the town won the first Glor na nGael competition in 1962. I trust you will find your parents bearing up well under their growing years.

Hoping to visit the Convent at the weekend and with God's blessing on you future work,

Yours very sincerely,
Tomas O'Fiaich
Cardinal Archbishop of Armagh

The last time I saw the Cardinal he was saying Mass for the sick of the Diocese. He looked so tired that I didn't go to talk to him. He was a man who wore himself out in the service of others. He will always be remembered in Cuan Mhuire for his great goodness and outstanding support, his simplicity, his sense of humour, and total genuineness."

On the 29th June1984, Sr Consilio with twelve long term recovering members of the Athy house, arrived in Newry to start the third Cuan Mhuire, which with a lot of hard work has thrived ever since. The first two people to welcome them with food and gifts were from the Protestant community which augured well for the future. Ever since, persons from all faiths and communities have been part of the Newry Cuan Mhuire.

Dr James Kavanagh, then auxiliary Bishop of Dublin, had this to say: "The extraordinary opening of a Cuan Mhuire house in Northern Ireland is an indication of the sort of growth which, under God will continue, and which will demand a grouping of people around Sr Consilio, who will be able to keep the different Cuans true to her initial inspiration."

By 1990, the buildings in Cuan Mhuire Athy had become obsolete. They were far too small to meet the needs of the ever growing number of people seeking help. Furthermore, they were in dire need of repair. After expert advice and consideration, it was decided that the most advisable course of action was to construct an entirely new building. This work was commenced on October 9th 1990. A committee was formed under the Chairmanship of Eoin Ryan SC to help raise funds for the new purpose-built complex.

At a reception held in the Mansion House, Dublin on October 31st 1990 to launch the fund raising, Sr Consilio had this to say: *"This evening we have gathered here about the building of a house. Cuan Mhuire is of course much more than a house; it is all about an awareness of the dignity and eternal value of each and every human being. From this awareness comes a deep respect for the person. I have no answers for the world's problems, or indeed for our country's problems, but it seems to me that these problems have a great deal to do with a lack of respect and with an unawareness of the unique value of each human being. Much of what we experience today bears witness to that.*

Our gift in Cuan Mhuire is that we have a glimmer of the fact that each person is made to the Image and Likeness of God Himself. Each person is beyond price. Any one person is more precious than all this world's goods put together. It doesn't matter how broken or bruised or even aggressive the person coming to the door is; that person cannot be written off as 'hopeless' or 'no good'. We know that each person has within himself/herself all that is needed for a happy, contented, useful life, if only he/she can get in touch with it.

That is what Cuan Mhuire is all about, - learning to live at a deep inner level - getting in touch with, and living from the unlimited capacity for goodness, love and truth that is within each one of us. As we build the new Cuan Mhuire in Athy, we will more importantly be building people. Already, after just three weeks, I can see twenty four members of our Cuan Mhuire family being transformed as they discover their gifts and talents on the site. I have no doubt but that by the time this building is complete, at least two hundred people will have found new hope and heart, and will have learned many skills or found the courage and confidence to return to skills they already had, but just couldn't use because of inner fear, turmoil, and despair in their lives. This evening I ask for your support for those whose lives are temporarily broken - the sick, the lonely, the rejected from all walks of life.

When I was young I told my father that I would like to have a house, a green field and a big family. When I told him I was joining the Sisters of Mercy he said: 'What about your house, your field and your big family?'. Little did I know then that the house and big family I wanted would become far too big for me to take care of on my own, and that is why I am counting on people like yourselves to come to my aid."

Because of the enormous cost involved in the building of the new Cuan Mhuire various fund raising activities were initiated - one such activity was the release of a single record in March 1992. "Side A" of the single was entitled Desiderata - this world famous piece of verse was found in Old St Paul's Church in Baltimore, USA in 1692. The words powerfully recited by film star John Hurt, encapsulate the Cuan Mhuire philosophy:

> THEREFORE BE AT PEACE WITH GOD
> WHATEVER YOU CONCEIVE HIM TO BE...
> AND WHATEVER YOUR LABOURS AND
> ASPIRATIONS IN THE NOISY CONFUSION OF
> LIFE, KEEP PEACE WITH YOUR SOUL...
> WITH ALL ITS SHAM, DRUDGERY AND BROKEN
> DREAMS, IT IS STILL A BEAUTIFUL WORLD...
> BE CAREFUL, STRIVE TO BE HAPPY.

The work which was started in October 1990 came to fruition when Cuan Mhuire's new, impressive, purpose-built Treatment and Rehabilitation Centre in Athy was blessed by Most Reverend James Kavanagh DD, and officially opened by Sr Sebastian Cashen, Mother General of the Sisters of Mercy, on Trinity Sunday

June 14th 1992. The ceremony was attended by hundreds of past residents, friends and benefactors of all the Cuan Mhuire centres. This modern, purpose-built, red brick building, with its beautiful courtyards and fountains can accommodate one hundred and fifty people. It is one more monument to the workmanship and dedication of Sr Consilio's brother Johnny, and his talented team.

With Cuan Mhuire centres established in Leinster, Munster and Ulster it was not surprising that Sr Consilio now turned her attention to the needs of the people of Connaught.

In the summer of 1993, while she was at home in Rockchapel, she happened to meet a local priest, Fr Timmy Curtin. He talked to her about Moyne Park, Coolarne, County Galway. The Sacred Heart Fathers had purchased it from the Sisters of Charity in 1975, but it was once more vacant and on the market. Fr Timmy felt it would be an ideal place for a Cuan Mhuire. Not long afterwards, Sr Consilio was on her way to Dublin when she got a call on the car phone - a Sacred Heart priest was ringing to ask if she would be interested in Coolarne House. She wasn't interested as Cuan Mhuire had a lot on hand at the time - the new Cuan Mhuire in Athy had to be paid for, there was a Transition House in Dublin and it needed total reconstruction. However, more from a sense of courtesy than conviction she said she would take a look at it.

She arrived for "the look around" at 7.40 am the following morning. She says that immediately she set foot there, she knew in her heart she was meant to be there. A deal was negotiated with the Sacred Heart Fathers, and on the following St. Patrick's Day, March 17th 1994, Sr Consilio and her little band of volunteers - Jackie Bozman, Mary Falvey, Maria Finnegan, Sheila Clinch, Chris Hilton, Donal Quigley, Dermot Ryan, Christy Smart, and the late Dr Pat McCarthy, Michael McTiernan, and Michael Sheehan took up residence in the new Cuan Mhuire. Scarcely had they landed when the first person came seeking admission, and he was quickly followed by many others.

"Coolarne House", later known as "Moyne Park" and today as "Cuan Mhuire", is a solidly constructed mansion situated fifteen miles from Galway City. The house itself is imposing and so too are its magnificent iron entrance gates, the picturesque stone gate lodge and the long curving avenue, with trees of every description on either side. If the house is impressive, much more so is the work that takes place within its walls. Here, we see a group of dedicated people who live at a deep inner level; people who strive to discover in themselves, and help others to discover their own inner giftedness, goodness and gentleness.

Cuan Mhuire Coolarne, needed major reconstruction work. This was commenced in October 1997. Since then a new twenty two bed Detoxification Unit, a fifty bed Treatment Centre, a new kitchen and dining room have been added. In addiction a separate building consisting of sixteen units and designed to accommodate forty people has been constructed.

This purpose-built Treatment Centre is the admiration of all who see it. It speaks volumes of the care with which the builder - once again Sr Consilio's brother, Johnny and members of the Cuan Mhuire family took with every detail from the foundation stone to the final plaque which was unveiled on the Feast of the Annunciation, March 25th 2000. The new building was officially opened by Bobby Molloy TD, Minister for State at the Department of the Environment, and Blessed by Most Rev Michael Neary DD. As with all Cuan Mhuire houses it is dedicated to the Immaculate Heart of Mary.

The concept of "Teach Mhuire" was formed in Sr Consilio's mind many years ago. She was aware that each year approximately eight hundred Dublin people take part in the Cuan Mhuire Treatment and Rehabilitation Programme at Athy, Bruree, Newry and Galway. Sr Consilio saw that these people needed support and "after care" when they had completed their recovery programme. She was also keenly aware of the need to provide support and counselling for their families. With this in mind, Cuan Mhuire Teoranta set about acquiring a house in Dublin's inner city.

Just then O'Brien's Hotel, 38/39 Lower Gardiner Street, Dublin 1 came on the market and was purchased by Cuan Mhuire. Later, when the former owner - Mrs O'Brien, heard of Sr Consilio's involvement, she was amazed as she had been making a novena to Our Lady of Good Counsel at the Augustinian Priory, St. John's Lane that "the right person" would acquire the property. Mrs

O'Brien was quick to make the connection between Our Lady of Good Counsel and the name Sr Consilio. The late Archbishop of Canterbury, Dr Ramsey, was once asked if he believed in coincidences. His reply was that experience had taught him to expect "God instances rather than coincidences".

No sooner had Cuan Mhuire acquired the property than Sr Consilio set out in her usual "all stops out" fashion to provide the much needed services. A complete overhaul operation was called for. For over two years a group of skilled and unskilled workers, who had recovered in the various Cuan Mhuires, did trojan work. Sr Maureen O'Sullivan did the cooking. Michael Ward did the overseeing and eventually the project was complete. Today it is a beautiful building with every modern convenience and comfort. It was officially opened by Liz O'Donnell TD, Minister for Housing and Urban Development on September 25th 1995, and blessed by Bishop James Kavanagh DD.

"Teach Mhuire" is a new venture for Cuan Mhuire. It provides first class, short-term, alcohol and drug free residential accommodation for persons in the transition stage, as they move from any of the Cuan Mhuire treatment centres into new communities, or back to their own communities. It also uses the services of addiction counsellors who cater for the counselling needs of residents, non-residents and family members. AA, NA, Women for Sobriety and After Care meetings are held there each week. No matter how busy their schedules, Sr Helen makes time and travels from Athy to facilitate the Tuesday night After Care meeting, while Sr Consilio takes two groups on Thursday night. Persons wishing to undergo treatment in any of the Cuan Mhuires can attend at Teach Mhuire on Mondays for assessment.

To-date, many thousands have passed through its doors. Some have come for "one-to-one" counselling or group therapy. Others have come to stay for a brief period until they have acquired their own accommodation. Others still, drop into the coffee-bar for a "cuppa",or simply to relax and have a chat in the company of fellow travellers on the road to recovery.

Seeing the havoc, the pain, the misery and the destruction caused by drug addiction in our country, Cuan Mhuire decided to open a separate twenty one-bed unit for the detoxification, recovery and rehabilitation of young persons suffering from drug addiction. This new unit was opened in Athy in 1996.

Cuan Mhuire put in place its own programme tailored to meet the special needs of young people suffering from drug addiction. To date this programme has been highly successful. Over a period of no less than fourteen weeks, the young people discover their real selves, their purpose in life and an understanding of the evil and destruction caused by drug abuse. They also get an insight into the reasons why they used drugs in the beginning, and come to terms with the steps they have to take, and the changes they have to make, in order to be able to let go of the patterns that led them into the drug world. As the weeks go by they manage to get in touch with the pain they had hoped to kill with these drugs, and they learn how to live out the pain and deal with it in a non destructive way. From people who believed they were the lowest of the low, certain they were always going to be failures, destined for a life of hell and misery, they, little by little, begin to discover their value and their worth as human beings. They begin to experience their inner goodness and giftedness, their ability to live normal, happy, contented lives, becoming aware of the fact that God created us all equal with unlimited capacities for life and living. Being on the road to recovery makes a huge impact on a person's self image and feeling of self worth.

Self discipline has a big part to play in the recovery of the young drug addict. In fact, without self discipline there is no recovery. Self discipline is a must because they have lived a totally undisciplined life since they started using drugs, and they have lived in a world of unreality and totally out of their minds with drugs. Recovery demands one hundred per cent attentiveness to the new way of life they are being asked to live. Those who are prepared to work hard and give the programme their very best effort make an amazing recovery. They put on weight, they become alive with a new zest for living as they begin to discover who they are - very special unique people, with a purpose in life. It is a real joy to watch them discover their real goodness as they give it away to each other.

Living in addiction is totally negative. It takes some time for new comers to become aware of how negativity has taken over their whole lives - it is the only thing they are used to. They more or less enjoy wallowing in their misery, being comfortable with the uncomfortable, afraid to let go of the familiar. Discovering the power of the positive is a huge step forward. When a group of people choose to be positive and live from it, even for one day, miracles happen. The power of their love and positivity creates great healing.

Sr Consilio says: *"The emphasis always has to be on the positive, and the importance of continuing to instil it in the group at all times has to be a priority among those who lead the group. To forget this could mean losing a number who would go back to their old ways, and return once again to the only life they know. Living in 'the now' is also very much part of life in Cuan Mhuire. It is the only reality there is. It is the only time one can live. It sets us free from the unnecessary, and usually pointless worry about the future. The present well lived leaves every yesterday a day well lived, and finds us ready for every tomorrow when it becomes today.*

Our whole programme is founded and grounded on unconditional Love. It is living at an inner deeper level - a soul level. It takes us away from the stress and strain of 'trying'. If trying were any good they would all be clean long ago. Trying is always at a head level, it is very limited and most people become very tired from trying. On the other hand a gentle attentiveness is very powerful whether it is to saying the single word in Meditation, or in listening to somebody sharing in the group, or to doing our own group work or work therapy. There is a peace, a calm a real force for good within us, and all around us - the power of God Himself. This is the key and the source of the success of our programme."

Sr Consilio is convinced of the need for physical exercise, especially for the younger people and recreation for all. This is evidenced by the new sports complex in Athy, the fine tennis court in Bruree, the gymnasia in Coolarne and Newry, and the fact that Sr Consilio was responsible for the establishment of an athletic and boxing club for local youths in the grounds of Cuan Mhuire Newry.

Young and old take part in weekly quizzes, scrabble, pool and other table games, while music and song are a regular occurrence in all the houses. In a word, one sees in Cuan Mhuire a family in the true sense, where people share, care, pray, play and work together as they discover their uniqueness, goodness, and real purpose in life.

As Sr Consilio walked from Cuan Mhuire to the convent in Athy her eyes rested on one of the town's eyesores. It was formerly the old Fever Hospital and now, in the early eighties, it was a derelict private residence. Sr Consilio saw that it could be brought back to life and used for people.

Around the same time Father Pat Murray was completing a course in Canada. He had been a constant visitor at Cuan Mhuire and was in tune with its spirituality. This house was purchased by Cuan Mhuire and refurbished in 1984/85 making it the beautiful place it is today. It was decided that it would become a house of prayer and growth with Fr Pat as Director, and henceforth it would be known as Galilee House.

Sr Consilio recalls that: *"I first met Fr Pat soon after moving to our first new Cuan Mhuire in Athy. He struck me at the time as a man who was searching for a deeper meaning in life. Some years later, Fr Pat visited me again. This time, he was home on holidays from Canada. He told me of the new life that had opened up for him since he began a course on PHR (Personality and Human Relations). Suddenly, I realised that he was in fact talking about the way of life that is being lived in Cuan Mhuire. This was very important for me. I knew at a deep level that the Cuan Mhuire way of life was the way I was meant to follow, but many others doubted it. Consequently, it was a wonderful re-assurance to discover that it was being taught and practised in other places with great success.*

Straight away, I asked Fr Pat if he would come to work for us, when he had finished his time in Canada. He agreed to do so. Six years later, Fr Pat came to Galilee to begin the sessions that have contributed so much to all our growth, and to the work of Cuan Mhuire.

I have never met anyone else who could compare with Fr Pat as a counsellor, as an educator - one who can call forth what is best and deepest in each person. He is a truly gifted priest and teacher. Hopefully, he will continue to work with us for many years to come."

Cuan Mhuire, as we have already seen, now has four rehabilitation and recovery centres - one in each of the four Provinces of Ireland, at Athy, Bruree, Galway and Newry. It has also established an inner city project in Dublin to assist in dealing with a wide range of individual and social problems. This has meant that there is now a greater need for trained personnel. Out of this need has developed a Diploma in Counselling at Galilee House of Studies. Initiated in 1992, the Diploma Course is open to all who meet the requirements, subject to availability of places. The Diploma meets the educational requirements of the IAAAC. It is accredited by the NAPCP.

The purpose of this course is to provide systematic training in counselling theory and practice at a level that will prepare participants to counsel in a variety of settings and to use various counselling approaches. In particular, it aims to train counsellors suited for the work of the Cuan Mhuire Rehabilitation Centres. To date approximately one hundred persons have been awarded the Diploma in Counselling from Galilee House. Many are employed in the Cuan Mhuire Centres; many others are employed by various agencies or have set up in private practice.

Cuan Mhuire, Bruree, Co Limerick

Cuan Mhuire, Bruree, Co Limerick – Reconstructed Courtyard

Cuan Mhuire, Bruree, Co Limerick Mass at the newly erected Grotto

Sr Consilio and Jim Donnan

John Moynihan   *Fr Dominic O'Neill*

Patsy Keane   *Fr Pat Murray*

Staff – Cuan Mhuire, Bruree, Co Limerick

Sean Moriarty and Muirne Hurley, on a visit to Cuan Mhuire, Bruree, during Muirne's reign as the Rose of Tralee

Sr Agnes and Gemma Wallace

Sr Maureen O'Sullivan

Pat and Lila Magee

Cuan Mhuire, Athy, Co Kildare

Cuan Mhuire, Athy, Co Kildare – Drug Unit

Cuan Muire, Newry, Co Down

Cardinal Tomás Ó Fiaich

Cuan Mhuire, Coolarne, Co Galway

The first group of Residents - Cuan Mhuire, Coolarne, Co Galway

Construction of the new Sports Complex, Cuan Mhuire, Athy, Co Kildare

Galilee House of Studies, Athy, Co Kildare

Official opening of Galilee House of Studies
Left to Right: Sr. Consilio, Bishop Kavanagh and Eileen O'Loughlin

First Graduates – 2 year Diploma in Counselling,
Galilee House of Studies, Athy, Co Kidlare

Sr Sebastian Cashen and Sr Consilio

Sheila Wall

Tony O'Mullane

Sr Maria Oman

Eileen Noonan

Sr Mary Cotter

Teach Mhuire, Dublin

Sr Helen Greene and Sr Consilio

Mary Ann and Paddy O'Connor

Left to Right: Sr Consilio, Nora Fleming, Sr Agnes and Mary Rose Teahan

Actor John Hurt, who did a voice-over on the Desiderata tape with Sr Consilio on the Pat Kenny Show 1992

Chapter 7

SPEAKING TO THE FAMILY

"The poor deserve preferential consideration regardless of their moral or personal condition. They are formed in the image and resemblance of God... to be His children. However, this image is tarnished and even insulted. But God protects and loves them... it follows that the primary recipients of the mission are the poor... and that their evangelisation is, above all, a sign and a proof of the mission of Jesus..."

Encyclical Letter Pope John Paul
Paragraph 56-60, January 22, 1991

There are not enough hours in the day to accommodate all those who want a word with Sr Consilio. There are not enough days in the year. The woman may have a huge heart and a huge commitment to the healing ministry which Cuan Mhuire represents, but few can appreciate the workload which she takes daily upon her shoulders. True, Sr Consilio has a band of loyal, dedicated and trusted staff, many of whom have been at her side for decades. They help to lighten the load of a punishing schedule of meetings, conferences, funerals and other commitments. Such is her reputation as a superb listener, comforter, friend and counsellor that everyone wants "a piece" of this woman. Many of her close friends have attempted, with little success, to get her to slow down, to "take it easy". Sr Consilio knows better than most, that giving of oneself means never holding back; it is the unconditional love which is never capable of saying "I will be there for you if it suits me" - rather, this woman believes that "fellow suffering and compassion" must be a reality in her daily life as much as it exists in the daily lives of those to whom she ministers. This is what marks Sr Consilio out as special - like the good Samaritan, this woman is moved to action, moved by the plight of others, and she can never fail to be so moved.

She would not have it any other way. Those who know her, understand. It must be seen in the context of one soul - a soul so intoxicated with love for God and His Mother that she seeks constantly to do the will of God - and in her own unique way to "die"' to those pleasures which are transient and illusory, and which are impediments to spiritual progress.

To "die" to oneself and to embrace and accept whatever pain and suffering comes our way out of love for God and our fellow human beings, trusting always that there is our Heavenly reward awaiting us. It is absolutely crucial to an understanding of what motivates Sr Consilio - this drive to get things done, to live the Gospel message of Love - that we understand and accept the rock-solid faith Sr Consilio places in God and Our Lady. For Sr Consilio, Our Lady is as real and as substantial as if she were standing beside her in the flesh. It is vital for us to appreciate this reality - then, and only then, do we approach an understanding of the importance which Sr Consilio attaches to every second of every moment of her life on this earth. And what a superb example of faith this woman gives out all around her. Many have returned to a spiritual way of life because of the profound effect which her faith has had upon them. It is as though many have come to believe from witnessing the strength of Sr Consilio's own faith. Sr Consilio's own words then, must be read with an eye to the overall context in which she speaks - as one who goes out in love and compassion, fortified by an unshakeable faith in God and Our Lady.

Welcoming New Arrivals

Sr Consilio's approach to those seeking admission to Cuan Mhuire is best summed up by the woman herself: *"When admitting a person, I always try to visualise myself at the other end of the phone or outside the door asking to be admitted. I know exactly what I would like to have said to me if I were in a desperate situation and condition and had nowhere to turn to, and maybe my last few pence dropping into the phone box. I always say to the other person what I would like said to me, and as best I can, I let the person know how welcome he/she will be, how glad I will be to see him/her. If I feel I have to ask a few questions, I keep it to a minimum. I never like being questioned myself; I like people to accept me as I am, and where I am at. The people who helped me most in life were the people who accepted me as I was and didn't try to change me. Very often, out of my gratitude for their love and acceptance, I changed myself."*

As Sr Consilio herself puts it: *"a capacity and a willingness to see beyond appearances"* is essential for those who work alongside her in the day-to-day running of Cuan Mhuire. *"When a person arrives at a Cuan Mhuire door, he or she may be aggressive, abusive, unshaven etc. Our gift in Cuan Mhuire is to be able to see beyond these appearances, beyond behaviour, beyond worldly standards, to be able to see the real person made to the image and likeness of God. To have a glimpse of the value, the worth, the uniqueness, the unrepeatability of each person. To come to understand that the person coming through the door is more valuable than all the treasures, all the material possessions, in the whole world. To realise the tremendous responsibility and very special calling that those of us who have been called to work in Cuan Mhuire undertake. This is what we need to be attentive to all the time. If we lose sight of this truth, we lose what is most fundamental to the Cuan Mhuire way of life. It takes a long time to understand that most people who come to the door are mentally, physically, emotionally, socially, and spiritually bankrupt. Many feel unwanted, useless, or full of fear. To have any idea of what it is like to be in this person's shoes, we must see ourselves outside rather than inside the door. "*

Cuan Mhuire as a Community

The Cuan Mhuire centres take the form of the Christian family, or little communities of the people of God. Each centre is one self-contained community of persons, who, for the time being, live, work, and pray together, nevertheless allowing each person his or her own space. There is no distinction on the basis of status. Some have leadership qualities, others have different qualities and talents. All eat together, the same food, in the same dining room. Each person contributes to the daily running of the centre. In this way - in undertaking a task for others, each regains a sense of responsibility, self-esteem, self confidence and love for others and for self. Each person is encouraged to give without seeking a reward, and in this way to grow and recover from their addiction, from their urge to seek gratification, and the illusion of security in the addictive substance or behaviour. It is the road to maturity in the love of God. The Cuan Mhuire way of life endeavours to facilitate each person in achieving life abundantly. To achieve peace, each person needs to discover a real contentedness within himself/herself - the "Immortal Diamond" of which Thomas Merton writes. To discover one's own essential goodness, or as St Paul puts it: "so that being rooted and grounded in love, you may be able to comprehend with all the saints, what is the breadth, the length, the height and depth, and to know Christ's love which surpasses knowledge in order that you may be filled unto all the fullness of God."

How Sr Consilio sees her role in Cuan Mhuire

Almost forty years on, Cuan Mhuire continues to grow and flourish. With houses in each province, a transition house in Dublin and Galilee House of Studies in Athy, the demands on Sr Consilio mean a punishing schedule of appointments, visits and funerals which are a constant source of anxiety to those closest to her. *"Cuan Mhuire gave me the opportunity to live the way Jesus Christ said we ought to live. It certainly gave me a chance every day to love my neighbour as myself. It gives me freedom to sit at the same table, share the same meals, enjoy the same way of life as all those who choose to come and live life with us. Our philosophy is that Cuan Mhuire is first, and above all, for those people whom nobody else wants or nobody else is prepared to help. People of every colour, creed and class are welcomed daily at our doors. It is our privilege to welcome Jesus Christ to our doors every time somebody comes for help. There are no questions about what they have, or what they can afford to pay. All that is expected is a willingness to do the best they can at the time to get well and begin a new life. It is our gift in Cuan Mhuire that we see beyond appearances and behaviour. We have a tiny glimmer of the value and the dignity of a human being. In Cuan Mhuire the person finds a comprehensive rehabilitation and treatment programme which gives him or her a reason for living, for enjoying and benefiting from each day as if it represented a whole lifetime."*

Faith - Belief

Sr Consilio continues: *"Unfortunately in today's climate even though many profess to be Christians or Catholics, they have grown up without any "real beliefs". Materialism has no doubt taken over so many people's lives, they live completely in a world of illusion that inevitably disappoints them at every turn leaving them disillusioned, distressed, with no faith and very little hope. In their dilemma - having no Spiritual dimension in their lives, they search for some such experience in drugs. They are like the man searching for his car keys under the lamp post. His friend comes along and sees him searching and says: 'Jack are you looking for something?' Jack replies: 'I am looking for my car keys.' After searching for about five minutes to no avail, the friend says: 'Jack where did you lose them, they are not here.' Jack says: 'About two hundred yards up the road.' 'And why are you looking here?' 'There is more light here,' replied Jack.*

Today people are looking in the bright lights for something that cannot be found there. They do not seem to understand that no amount of pleasure will make you happy. Happiness is deep down inside each one of us and can only be discovered by us as we give it away to each other.

Likewise, faith is a belief in the love, protection and care of a God who gave his only son to die on a cross for us - a God who has a special place for us for all eternity if we choose to go there. Without faith, life can be very meaningless, very lonely and can lead to hopelessness and despair. Faith of course is a gift, and those who fail to accept it have a much poorer hope of recovery. Living in Cuan Mhuire gives each one of us a golden opportunity of living our lives the way God wants us to live them, and becoming the beautiful people we are meant to be."

Her Love for Others

She will cajole, encourage and sometimes irritate family members - all in an effort to wake them up to the reality of their condition. One former resident recalls how during his time in Cuan Mhuire, he was wrestling with so many mixed emotions towards his own father. Sr Consilio took him aside one evening and asked him to imagine he was meeting face to face with his father. *"Tell him how you feel - let him hear it all, good and bad!"* This young man unburdened himself of many pent-up feelings and gradually came to a peaceful regret for the many things that had been lacking in his relationship with his father, but also a gratitude for the many positive acts of kindness his father had shown. The message - the essential truth - which those in recovery will inevitably come to understand, is that there is no such thing as the perfect parent or the perfect human being. As we come to a deeper understanding of our own limitations, we can allow others their imperfections without apportioning blame. Understanding and tolerance of others are essential ingredients of true love - an acceptance of people as they are, and not as we would like them to be. *"I really do love every one of them and they know it. I make lots of mistakes, but one thing I am constant about is my love for them. You must understand that many of these people have never felt loved in their whole lives. Sometimes, without justification, they have felt inadequate, they have felt that people just didn't care about them. While you or I might always have felt secure in our families, certain that we were loved for ourselves, many of these people didn't feel loved. Maybe they felt - rightly or wrongly - that a parent had a 'down' on them, or that others in the family were that much more appreciated and loved, and this feeling has never left them. The only time such people feel like you or I normally feel is when they have a few drinks or take some other mood altering drug. Then they feel accepted, loved and adequate. Love is the whole key, but sometimes they cannot accept that they are loved, even when they know it. They may even try to force you to reject them, to give up on them, to prove to themselves that they really are unlovable. But by perseverance one can build their trust, which is essential. Many of them also can't love other people. Some of them have never actually been in love in their whole lives and many probably should never have got married. I know several people who were married in an alcoholic haze, who don't even remember getting married."*

The Spiritual Aspect of Recovery

Sr Consilio continues: *"I am totally convinced of the importance of the spiritual aspect of recovery; without God we can do nothing, with Him all things are possible. I encourage those who are a long time away from the Sacraments to go to Confession. I make a point of telling the story of* the Prodigal son returning, and being truly welcomed by the father. I explain Confession to them in this context. I always encourage them to participate in the Family Rosary and to have devotion to Our Lady who is our main strength and support.

Our Lady has looked after us all down the years and She will do the same for them if thy ask Her. I also encourage them to go to Mass every day; it is only half an hour at most and can be of great benefit to them."

The Gift of Cuan Mhuire

"Of all the gifts and talents we bring with us to Cuan Mhuire, the greatest and the most important is our love.'Love blots out a multitude of sins'. We can have all the techniques and training in the world, and they all have their own importance, but if they are not founded and grounded on love they are only 'sounding brass and tingling cymbal'. Love is seeing the goodness in ourselves and calling it forth in others.

Our gift in Cuan Mhuire is that we have a tiny, tiny, glimmer of the value, the uniqueness, the beauty, the wonder of what it is like to be a human being. It is being attentive to this gift that makes Cuan Mhuire what it is today. This gift enables us to see beyond appearances and behaviour, and makes us aware of the fact that God created us all equal, unique and special; so special that nobody could be more special. Everyone whom we are privileged to welcome through our doors is to be seen as he or she is - not as they appear to be. Welcoming each person is like welcoming Jesus Christ himself or His Mother. Cuan Mhuire is in trust for that person exactly in the same way as it is in trust for you and me - more so if the person is at the time in greater need than we are. No one person at any time, or in any situation has the right to refuse admission to anybody who comes. However, there are times and rare situations where a number of responsible and caring people have to make choices. It is a huge responsibility to turn away somebody. Always be sure not to make any such decisions when you are upset or angry. These, above all other decisions are to be made out of your love, and it needs to be explained to the person who is not being admitted the reasons why he or she cannot stay at this time. Do all you can to get them placed or helped in a more suitable environment."

Unconditional Love

"The Cuan Mhuire way of living from within is based on unconditional love; giving without expecting anything in return. The only part of you or me that is capable of that kind of love is the part of us made like God Himself. If we give from our heads we expect something back, even a word of thanks. In practising unconditional love, we are practising living from our souls whether we are aware of it or not.

Unconditional love has a power all of its own: the power of God. Living from our unconditional love is like turning on the rotary mower to mow a meadow, while living at a head level is like trying to mow that same meadow with a hedge clippers, or, like turning on the power rather than trying to light up a city with a candle. It is all about discovering the Kingdom of God within; the hidden treasure in the Gospel. The treasure we can only discover as we give it away to others; the more we give away the more we have to give because it is connected to the Power of God Himself.

Because we have a glimmer of this boundless goodness and giftedness in each person, we know there is no such thing as a hopeless case."

Does she ever end up hating the addict?

"I don't hate anybody in the world. At times I may get upset but the fact remains that I look up to them and admire them. I just go on loving the people in Cuan Mhuire no matter what, and that's what they need. There is only one way to deal with an alcoholic...never give up on him. Total commitment to eternity is the only way."

"Loving the sinner while hating the sin", is therefore, very much at the core of Sr Consilio's beliefs. We do not forfeit the right to be respected, even when we behave in a manner that is objectionable or unacceptable. *"Of course there are occasions when a person may be advised that they do not seem to be embracing the Cuan Mhuire programme in an honest or sincere manner, and that perhaps they ought to leave and return when they are ready to do so."*

Each case is dealt with on its own merits and people who have returned to undertake a second course of treatment at Cuan Mhuire will readily admit that "this time around" they are much more sincere and honest in their approach to the programme.

People who Commit crimes

Some of those who seek help for alcohol or drug addictions at Cuan Mhuire have been in trouble with the law. Very often Cuan Mhuire is a place of last resort - the "Last Chance Hotel" as one newspaper called it - where a person is afforded a real opportunity to look at the reasons behind his or her addictive behaviour. What modern therapy nowadays terms a "dysfunctional" upbringing or environment, is often the root of the malaise which the addicted person feels can only be alleviated - albeit temporarily, and with adverse long-term effects - by recourse to alcohol and/or other drugs.

In the last analysis, many men and women have made a whole new beginning at Cuan Mhuire. Having discovered - perhaps for the first time in their lives - how precious they are in God's eyes, they have begun all over again, and have truly rehabilitated themselves. *"Immaturity is what causes most of the ills in the world - big and small, from family quarrels to wars. It is also responsible for physical illness. It is noteworthy that the majority (though not all) drug addicts, drug pushers and so-called drug barons come from deprived areas of Dublin and elsewhere. The message is that these inner city areas and large local authority housing estates are indeed deprived areas. Apart from the deprivation in individual families, through unemployment etc., the areas are also deprived of amenities particularly for children and young people. I remember many, many years ago when places like Ballymun were being built, my father who was just an ordinary farmer used to say over and over again: 'What chance will the young people who are born and grow up in these crowded places have in life? What difficulties will they have to cope with?' How right he was... Surely, if he, who was so far removed in every way from that scene could see the consequences, one has to ask the question, what were the politicians and the city planners doing? Would any of these people live in, or expect their own children to live in such conditions? Instead of blaming the young people who are the victims of their environment we ought to look at those who were the real cause of the situations that have arisen as a result of their actions.*

Prisons, as now operated, are obviously not the answer. The person who is, for whatever reason, a danger to himself or others may have to remain in custody, but a greater effort should be made to rehabilitate him or her. We are ourselves very much aware of how people's behaviour can change with rehabilitation. St Augustine said: 'You have made me for yourself O Lord and my heart will not rest until it rests in thee.' We are wounded through the consequences of original sin, through inheritances and through deprivation of love, security and so on, especially in our early childhood.

Often, people go the road of addictions as they seek to kill the pain of their woundedness. We need to seek wholeness - personal growth towards maturity in the fatherhood of God. Inner growth is slow; it is not easy, it requires grace, insight, prayer, meditation, help from others and given to others journeying with us. As St Paul puts it: 'The Spirit too, comes to the aid of our weaknesses, but in like manner, the Spirit also helps our weaknesses.'

The fact that the highest rate of crime is among the underprivileged, poorly educated and unemployed is telling us a lot about its basic cause. I have been in many courts over the past thirty seven years, and one look around the courthouse tells me that they are mainly places for unfortunate people, whose environment and background created problems for them in life since their very conception. Living and working in Cuan Mhuire for the past thirty seven years, and having listened to the inside stories of thousands of people, I can see very clearly that a person's childhood has a major part to play in his or her whole life. Children brought ·up in poor circumstances, where there is a lot of unemployment, where many have been unemployed all their lives, and where they have never experienced the sense of dignity and purpose one gets from going to work and earning a decent wage, are at a big disadvantage. Because of poor circumstances and lack of money, their children never enjoy many of the privileges enjoyed by the children of better off families. Very often, these parents have a poor understanding of the value of education. Very often too, they themselves escape into the temporary release offered by alcohol and drugs, forgetting that by so doing, they are making life miserable and unbearable at home for spouses and children.

It is easy to understand why teenagers, who themselves have no hope of employment, who have seen their parents before them unemployed, and who have very little else to do other than hang around the streets, often get involved in joy-riding, probably saying to themselves that 'this is the only way I will ever get a chance of driving a car.' They end up stealing in order to get for themselves the 'treasures' their apparently wealthier neighbours possess. This is by no means to condone the offence, but neither can we ignore what often appears to be the root cause."

Prisons Generally

Sr Consilio has visited prisoners in prison. She has accepted people into Cuan Mhuire who have been in trouble with the law from an early age - yet she would tell anyone who has ears to hear that the real prison we inhabit is that within ourselves - the prison of our own making. The story is told of how two former inmates of a Nazi extermination camp met up after many years. During a long conversation, one man asks the other one: "Can you forgive them for all they did to us?" "Never, never, never!" replies the second one. "In that case," says the first man "you're still in prison..." There are many who inhabit a prison without walls or bars. They are their own gaolers and until such time as they shake off the shackles of their old attitudes and beliefs, they remain in prison.

"My idea of prison would be a place where those who wish to change would have the opportunity to do so, and that they should do so under the guidance of people who have an understanding of the dignity of each human being, people who believe that underneath all the bad behaviour there is a beautiful person, waiting to come forth - a person with unlimited capacities for goodness. Whether we know it or not, we are all made to the image and likeness of God Himself. God never made junk. To help people to change involves a lot of hard work, and a lot of unconditional love, but it is possible and it can be done. We are all human beings and for recovery we have to be treated as such. It is no use treating the body - the whole person has to be taken into account - the body and soul. "

The poor self-image of many who come to Cuan Mhuire

Self-loathing is not too strong a term to describe the point which many people reach in their addictions.The "mountain" seems impossible to climb and even the smallest step out of the mire is so painful. Poor self-esteem - a negative view of oneself - will be alleviated in the short term by recourse to alcohol or other drugs - but it returns with a vengeance. The Cuan Mhuire programme aims at helping the addicted person to come to see himself or herself in a more positive light. The problem is in the person, not in the world around him. Once he makes this discovery, he will never see things in quite the same negative way again: *"The majority of people who come to the door, come feeling unwanted, having gone down the road of despair and misery, having lost hope in God, themselves and everybody else. Here, in Cuan Mhuire they build up a great trust in God and Our Lady. Very many have not been practising whatever religion they belong to for many years, but very seldom do they leave Cuan Mhuire without returning to their religion. There is no pressure on anyone but it can be seen that most people who are making a good recovery go to Mass and pray. Anyone who tries prayer finds out that it works. We handed Cuan Mhuire over to Our Lady and She has looked after us. When the addict feels he is worthwhile, when he feels he has a value, he is on the road to recovery."*

The Role of Cuan Mhuire
in the Education of Young People

One thing that strikes the visitor to Cuan Mhuire is the warm welcome that is always reserved for children. Indeed many of those who have recovered in Cuan Mhuire will often return to say "hello" to Sr Consilio and other family members, and they are encouraged to bring their children along. There is always the warmest welcome for children. There is the opportunity for older teenagers to undertake voluntary work in one of the Cuan Mhuire houses and many do so every year. This they thoroughly enjoy; it gives them an insight into the working of the centres and allows them to get to know the residents there.

There is also an "outreach" programme. Following extensive

discussions with teachers and parents, a programme was constructed to maximise the potential and impact of the message regarding the dangers of addiction. The programme consists of a series of meetings with students and parents in the school environment. Students and parents are taught the dangers and consequences of the misuse of addictive substances. Under the guidance of a qualified counsellor, each addictive drug is discussed and evaluated for damaging effects, both in the short and the long term. Audio and visual aids are used to enhance this message. By far the most powerful and influential part of the programme is the contribution made by recovering addicts themselves. In each school, three recovering addicts share their experiences of drugs with students and parents, emphasising the effect that drug abuse has had on their lives, and the consequences for them in physical, emotional, legal, social and career terms. At all times this group is supervised by a qualified Addiction Counsellor who can clarify any issues that may arise. Research and feedback from the schools shows that these sessions have a very positive impact on young people. This is evidenced by a one hundred per cent call back rate to the schools visited, and by the fact that frequently, sessions continue in an informal manner long after the allotted time.

Recognising also the role that parents have to play in their childrens' education, and the fact that parents too, lack a basic understanding of drug related issues, it was decided to extend the programme to all parents in an effort to encourage discussion at a family level. While the implementation of this part of the programme requires great commitment and time, the results have been exceptional. Research shows that one of the biggest reasons for parents' anxiety is their lack of understanding of the drug culture and of the signs and symptoms of drug abuse. Working with young people, Sr Consilio says: *"I am amazed at the number who have gone all through school and yet are unable to read and write. This places them at a dreadful disadvantage. We, in Cuan Mhuire, conscious of this, provide literacy and numeracy classes with the result that many learn to read and write for the first time while they are in treatment, and this in turn helps their self confidence and self worth."*

Advice to Parents

"I would emphasise our immortal souls - the difference between living from our inner beings rather than from our intellects only. I encourage my nephews and nieces to give, to care and to share. Although I realise the importance of passing exams I don't over emphasise them. It is important for persons to understand that every child has a need to feel loved. By 'love' I mean being seen, heard, believed and accepted as he or she is - and each child needs to have a safe place. When these needs are not met by people who are significant to the child, such as parents, older brothers or sisters, guardians or teachers, the child is wounded. While there is no such thing as perfect parents, a lot can be done by parents who understand their children. Children require parents to be parents; each child has to be seen as unique, special - with his or her own gifts. Having too high expectation of children can put terrible pressure on them, and they will end up always expecting too much from themselves and that is a burden too heavy to bear."

The Role of Parents
in the fuller Education of their Children

"It is vital to realise the importance childhood has on a person's future life. It is most important for a child to know that he is loved for himself and is not in competition with anyone else. Parents and teachers play a very big part in fostering self-esteem in children. In my own case, I grew up in a home where we were repeatedly told, and where we believed, that we were 'good'. In my mother's vocabulary we were always 'good girls' and 'good boys'. Likewise, my father told me many times that I was good. I believed them and that belief stood me in great stead all my life. Be sure to tell your children that they are 'good'. If their behaviour is not acceptable, always separate the behaviour from the person. 'How can a good child like you behave is such a manner?' and so on. People should be encouraged to be themselves, not what other people want them to be. To be encouraged to develop their talents and gifts to the best of their ability. Allow them to be themselves. Encourage, support and help them. Accept them as they are and they will blossom. If you push them to achieve, you over-burden them, and very often they end up totally dissatisfied with themselves. Nothing they achieve will be enough, they will want more and will be continually dissatisfied with themselves."

Friendship

"Love and friendship are what life is all about. Friendship has been my life's blood. Cuan Mhuire is all about friendship and fellowship. It is its main source of healing. The love that is generated in each group is far more important for the life of the group than anything else. We can have all the techniques, all the group therapy in the world, and while these all have their place, without love, as it says in the Gospel: 'They are only sounding brass and tingling cymbals'."

To What Does Sr Consilio attribute the continuing success of Cuan Mhuire?

As has already been noted, Sr Consilio places all her trust and faith in God and Our Lady. When she speaks of her Patroness, she is speaking of a special friend - one who has always been, and will always be there for her and for Cuan Mhuire. It is truly a faith which has moved mountains and which allows for not a moment's despair. For every problem Our Lady will intercede and provide a solution. For Sr Consilio, Our Lady is indeed, the Mother of God, who has showered her blessings on her and Cuan Mhuire since the first days of its existence. And so, she answers the question "To whom do you attribute your success?" as follows :*"To Our Lady and the Lord Himself; to my parents who loved me as I was. They made no demands on me. They gave me plenty of time and space to grow up. They allowed me be myself and gave me the opportunity to become responsible at an early age. They stood by me when times were difficult. They always had an open door in case I wanted to return home. They gave me a positive outlook on life; trusted me; never lectured me; or doubted my actions. To my brothers and sisters who have always helped me in every way they could. To Mother Mary of the Sacred Heart - my Superior when Cuan Mhuire first began. She continued as my parents had begun. Her great trust and support was a tremendous help. To the Trustees - men of great character, generosity and foresight; extraordinary people of faith and trust. They were, and are, a real blessing and the backbone of Cuan Mhuire. To the many dedicated people who came and worked day and night to keep our houses going, and who continue to do so to this present day. Without these dedicated and committed people who are the real core - the heart and the soul of*

Cuan Mhuire - we could not continue. The generosity of our Irish people who never fail to support us and keep the dinner on the table. To the Manager of the Sr Consilio Fund, who was appointed in the early days by the late Ned Nolan. To all our Fund Raisers who year after year promote our cause. It would be nice to name them all, but I have decided not to name names, lest even one of these helpers, past or present, should inadvertently be forgotten.

To Sr Sebastian Cashen who, as Mother General, gave me every support and help. She is a great woman and a wonderful friend to Cuan Mhuire. To Sr Paul Cosgrave, who was for a time my superior in Cuan Mhuire. She was always so genuine, gentle and trusting.

To all the Athy Sisters of Mercy. If I had life all over again, it is the Community I would want to join. To my noviceship training. It was a wonderful formation. I didn't fully appreciate it until recent years, when I found myself faced with the responsibility of putting together a programme for young people who are addicted to drugs. Then I saw clearly the value of our noviceship training, with its emphasis on self-discipline, prayer, living in the present, being positive, and the total use of time whether for work or recreation.

Women and the Priesthood,
Gay Rights, Divorce, Contraception and Abortion

Sr Consilio has always been at pains to emphasise her particular area of ministry - that of a life alongside the addicted, the homeless and those who have been ostracised by society."*My essential activity,*" she says "*is to journey with others.*" To this end, she does not question others about their religious persuasion, their sexual orientation or marital status. She gets on with the task of helping those who seek her help, to grow to be the beautiful people she believes they were created to be. Ask her for her views on controversial "Church" issues and her reply is simple:"*I accept the teaching of the Church.*" She always stresses the utmost respect for the dignity of each and every person with whom she comes in contact. There is no ambivalence, no duplicity and no false posturing about this woman. She calls it as she sees it, and gets on with the job on hand.

The Nun's Life Today

"It is very different in many ways. Years ago, when I entered the convent, we were told 'Keep the Rule and the Rule will keep you'. Blind obedience was the order of the day. The superior was always right.

Today, it is very different. I see obedience as listening from within and being ready and willing to follow God's plan as revealed to us from moment to moment. Poverty for me, is being available for others, having little or no time for oneself. Chastity is being free to love the whole world, seeing and being attentive to living from the goodness within oneself, and seeing the goodness, and calling it forth in others. Having the freedom to devote one's whole life to others, not being tied to one person or to one family.

In the past there were very large communities and all the sisters in any given house were mainly involved in the same work - nursing, teaching or housekeeping. It was organised so that all the sisters spent a lot of time together at community exercises and recreation. Most of the work was done in the houses or schools, and sisters had every opportunity to give each other a lot of help and support. It is very different now; communities are very much smaller. Sisters work very different hours in many different locations; they have very little time together and they have many different interests. Most of the decisions as to what work they ought to do is left to the sisters themselves. They have to take far more responsibility for their own lives, their own work, and their own needs. On the whole, I feel religious life today is more challenging, especially as the example of total, life-long commitment and dedication is more needed than ever before, in a world that is falling apart at the seams because of a lack of such commitment in marriages and families. These changes have come about as a result of all the changes that are taking place all around us. We have to move with the times; more important still we must keep in mind that many of these changes have come from a return to the spirit of the foundress, rather than from keeping to the letter of the law. The foundress of the Mercy Order, Mother Catherine McAuley, was always before my mind and what she did for the poor was a great example to me."

Work

"My work is my life and my life is for others. God looks after my needs. I don't have to worry about that. My essential activity is to journey with others."

Why she did not marry

"Just one man, one home and one family would not have satisfied me. I would want to be helping this one, that one, and the other one, and no man could be expected to put up with that."

Her Mission in Life

"My mission in life is to live the way God wants me to, and to help others to do likewise".

Chapter 8

PERSONAL EXPERIENCES

"I waited patiently for the lord;
he inclined to me and heard my cry,
he drew me up from the desolate pit,
out of the miry bog,
and set my feet upon a rock,
making my steps secure."

Psalm 40

The story is told of how a farmer found an eagle's egg and put it in the nest of one of his barnyard hens. The eaglet hatched with the chicks and grew up with them. All his life, the eaglet believed he was a chicken. He clucked and cackled just like all the other chickens and hens. From time to time he would thrash his wings and fly a few feet into the air. The years passed until, one day, the eagle, now quite old, looked up and saw a magnificent bird hovering above him in the sky. It glided gracefully with the powerful air currents with scarcely any effort. The old eagle looked up in awe: "Who is that?" he asked an old hen. "Why, that's the eagle - the king of the birds. He belongs in the sky." The eagle lived and died a chicken, for that's what he thought he was.

The world is full of eagles who never realise their full potential, many of them, just like the eaglet in the above story, have been deeply wounded in their childhood years and have lost faith in their ability to meet the many challenges which are put in their way. Quite literally the addict is a person who stops growing. Every difficult or painful situation becomes an occasion for a turning away from reality - an increased dependency upon chemical substances. There is no maturing - there is no self discipline - and things go from bad to worse, as the addict attempts to manipulate external events, in order to satisfy his internal needs. This leads to even greater chaos. Because of the progressive nature of his addiction, the person finds that his need for the security or anaesthetic of the addiction increases and he is caught up in a vicious cycle. So many men and women lose their lives to chemical addiction. They never grow to be the people they were created to be, with all the potential they possess. They die without ever becoming aware of their goodness and their giftedness. They are not "bad" people and those who are fortunate enough to find Cuan Mhuire, and to open themselves to change, come to see themselves, for the good and decent people they are. It can be a long and painful journey, but it is one which is well worth making. And always - the question to be asked of oneself will be: "Why do I do these things?" Many have come to realise that addiction is really anything that is done in an attempt to change reality - to alter or dilute interior moods and feelings by taking substances which makes the person feel - albeit only temporarily - "well" or "happy" or "above it all". In the end, as most addicts will confirm, it is enough simply to put oneself into a state of mental oblivion. The "fun" and the "kicks" have long since gone. All that remains is the feeling of emptiness. Some stories in this chapter are the personal accounts of men and women who have made that most important of journeys - the journey back to oneself. They live and breathe today because of the new beginning they found in Cuan Mhuire, where so many have been rescued from oblivion. Other stories tell of the personal experiences of people who lived and worked with Sister Consilio over the past four decades.

Sr Dominic recollects

I feel that I was responsible for introducing Sr Consilio to the Sisters of Mercy, Athy. I was waiting for her at the railway station in Portlaoise on her first visit. I knew immediately that she was the type of person who would fit in well with our community, and I hoped that before the day was out, she would have made the decision to enter our Novitiate.

However, we had to wait some weeks before we got the good news that she was coming. When eventually, she entered on 8th September 1959, she was well received by all. She settled into the Novitiate quite quickly. Being a trained nurse, she was much appreciated, especially by the senior sisters - many of whom she looked after.

When she was professed, she came to St Vincent's Hospital and was appointed on the nursing staff. There were approximately three hundred patients in St Vincent's at the time. The building was very old, but we were assured that in a short time a new hospital would be built, and so it was.

Sr Consilio was a wonderful help to me. She was most capable of fitting into any situation. She had a great understanding of the patients. Some were handicapped and not capable of looking after themselves, but with help and guidance they were of assistance to the staff and old people. Sr Consilio worked for a while in the kitchen. She had a real flair for cooking, so she always found ways of varying the meals. At that time, we were limited as to what we could spend; our budget was always stretched. She was an expert at jam making and it was wonderful to see all she could do with very little facilities.

Sr Consilio did an excellent job in the Maternity Unit where there were thirty mothers. All had great confidence in her and some even gave her name to their new born babies. She had a real interest in the "men of the road". She always took special care of them when she was working on that side of the house. It was there that she got to know, and understand the lads who were over-fond of drink. She helped them in many ways - spiritually as well as temporarily. When she was at the height of her work in St Vincent's, the

Superior re-called her to St Michael's Convent to help out in the Bursary. Their gain was our loss. I was upset to see her going as it was a time when I badly needed her to help me. She had been two years in St Vincent's. Some of the men who needed her help went down to the convent every day to have a word with her. She then saw the need of a place to keep them overnight, so she arranged with her superior and got the use of a place near the Convent. That is where the real Cuan Mhuire started. She did wonderful work down there with her counselling and spiritual advise. Many were reconciled and gained sobriety.

Sr Consilio had wonderful courage and of course her faith in Our Lady got her over many hurdles. When building the new Cuan Mhuire, her helpers and herself worked very hard to meet all financial expenses. All this could not have happened were it not for Sr Mary of the Sacred Heart and many members of the Community who gave her great support. There were many successful patients and they in turn started helping others.

While in St Vincent's, apart from her nursing duties, she took on young lads of fourteen and fifteen years of age, who were constantly getting into trouble. She advised them and prepared them for interviews etc. On one occasion a young lad let her down. When his employer rang up to make complaints about him, her reply was: *"We were all young once and often young people get into mischief."* Some of the lads qualified as mechanics or gained trades and did wonderfully well. These were lads who otherwise would have had no chance in life.

God created Sr Consilio to do some definite service for Him, and that is what she is doing. She could never have managed were it not for the help of Liam Tiernan, who put his car at her disposal and was always a man whom she could trust regarding the business of the place. He sacrificed a good job to give time to the work of Cuan Mhuire here in Athy and many other places. God has been very good to him in giving him the strength to carry on at his work. He has great influence over the people who come for treatment and Sr Consilio can always depend on him.

I wish her good luck and success in all her undertakings. She is a very brave woman and a great Sister of Mercy.

Sr Cecilia of the Convent of Mercy, Athy writes

It was my privilege to be with Sr Consilio in the final years of her Novitiate. Normally, the Novice Mistress (as she was then called) "directed" the novices, but in my case it was Sr Consilio who lead the way. She opened my eyes to a practical and inspiring way of living out to Gospel values. As far as she was concerned, help was to be given where, and when, needed. This might be a little chiropody, a vitamin injection, a pick-me-up tonic, or helping someone to start a car. Added to that, there was no distinction as to time, place or person. Of course, we never thought that she could be tired and somehow she never was! She was ever-ready. She could "do all things", drawing strength as she did from the only real Source. Our Lady was her constant companion and Sr Consilio was gifted with the assurance that Mary, God's Mother, was never known to leave anyone who called on her, unaided.

Sr Consilio would be the first to acknowledge that she owes a debt of gratitude to her wonderful parents - Maurice and Mary Agnes, and to every member of her family. That is where it all began.

Ag Criost an siol, ag Criost an Fomhar -
In lothlainn De go dtugtar sinn -

Recreation Time, by Sr Colette

I entered the congregation of the Sisters of Mercy in Athy on the 8th September 1962. I was fortunate to have as companion Sr Gabriel Quirke who came from Oola, Co Limerick. We both arrived in the Convent around three pm and were warmly welcomed by the Community Sisters, Junior Professed (then called black Novices, due to the fact that they had temporary vows and wore black veils), and the Novices. Among the group of "juniors" was Sr Consilio. She gave me a big hug and a warm welcome. She teased me by saying: *"Thank God you have come, because we have been hearing about this lovely girl for so long that it is good to get a look at you."* Since I attended the local Primary and Secondary Schools, I was well known to the Sisters and in particular to the Novice Mistress, Sr Cecilia, who had taught me music.

When Sr Consilio came to know me better, as we journeyed through the various stages of formation, she realised that the "lovely girl" had many flaws. I would, for example, use some expressive language when I missed the ball at tennis. Then, with a broad grin, Sr Consilio would remind me of "the perfect one" who was held up to them as a Model. Sr Consilio herself enjoyed tennis, but the religious dress of the day greatly hampered her style. Everything that could be rolled up or pinned up, was put in place, but still the veil kept getting in the way, not to mention the guimp which was always at an angle and a bit off side, never in the centre. Her manner of serving balls was a bit the same - you never knew where they were going to land. You were lucky if they were within the court as they were long and high, and could end up in the adjoining field or nearby trees. She had great dexterity and was equally good with the right or left hand. If you happened to be on the receiving end of her backhand swing you were in trouble as it came with mighty force and from any direction. She didn't win many matches, but her laughter and good humour brought new life to the group. After "recreation" we really felt re-created as we went to evening prayer with a song in our hearts thanking God for Sr Consilio.

Her ability to tell jokes and funny stories also added to the uplifting of our spirits. For some of us, loneliness would dampen our spirits at times, but this was never a problem for Sr Consilio.

She had left a home where she was dearly loved and where she had loved her family - now she could extend this love to the new Community. She often told the story of buying the indoor shoes. These were an essential part of a postulant's trousseau. Just as she was about to leave home for Athy on the morning she was entering the Convent, she took a last hurried look at the postulant's list. To her horror she realised that she had forgotten to purchase indoor shoes.The local shoe shop keeper was alerted at an early hour, but despite his best efforts, she landed in Athy with two left shoes - much to her own, and our amusement!

The 28th December - Feast of the Holy Innocents, was always a special day for novices in formation. One of the items on the agenda for the day was entertainment for the Community Sisters in the afternoon. Since singing was not Sr Consilio's forte, she focussed on drama. One of the highlights was Percy French's "Phil the Fluter's Ball". Little Miss Cafferty (Sr Consilio) arrived dressed to the nineties in her "Private Ass and Car" - an old wheelbarrow. As soon a she stepped on stage, without opening her lips, the audience went into gales of laughter and nothing was heard - not even the piano from then onwards. A play, without Sr Consilio was like a pub with no beer! Dry indeed.

On a more serious note I always turned to Sr Consilio for a word of advice and encouragement, as even at that stage she was a mature woman of common sense who had no time for petty trifles, and always had a heart for people both young and old, rich and poor, but in particular for the young men, unemployed and homeless who came to our doors seeking help. She not only gave them food, but she listened to their stories with a compassionate heart. This great love for such young people and their problems compelled her to do something for them, and with a faith that can move mountains, the support of her Superior - Sr Mary of the Sacred Heart, her community, her family and a few friends, a room for such people was given to her and Cuan Mhuire, Mary's Harbour became a reality. This was the mustard seed. Here people grow strong in faith and self awareness, knowing that their Heavenly Father loves and cared for them.

Sr Consilio had a dream, and with Mary's help water has been turned into wine, and many people share in the banquet of life once again.

As Sr Consilio herself would say: *"It is in God's hands and God will provide."* So, let us look to the future with hope for the new millennium and thank god for Sr Consilio.

My tribute to a larger-than-life Kerry woman, by Sister Peig Rice

To be asked to contribute my thoughts, experiences and knowledge of Sr Consilio is an honour, but also a daunting task. She is a woman of so many parts, including the ability to turn her hand to just about anything. She always has boundless energy with a perseverance and commitment to doing what she feels is of benefit to others, especially people with various problems and addictions. Her faith and trust in God and Our Lady is amazing. Her sense of humour and fun contribute to the unique character of this larger than life Kerry woman.

I first met Sr Consilio when I was a postulant back in 1959, when she visited Athy for the first time with the intention of joining the Sisters of Mercy. This she did some months later and since then my admiration and respect for her increases over the years, in spite the fact that we followed different ministries. She always turns up trumps at short notice, no matter who is in need. Her respect for all people, irrespective of class or creed is remarkable.

One thing we had in common before entering in Athy, was our Nursing Profession. We were older, more independent than our companions, so falling into line was difficult. However, in spite of the rules and regulations, we made our own fun and had many a laugh. Later we worked together in the local St Vincent's Hospital, caring for the elderly, taking turns at being on call for the Maternity Unit, and Sr Consilio also worked in the hospital kitchen as well as seeing to many other duties and needs.

It was at the hospital that she first got the feel for the "down and outs", especially men struggling with alcohol addiction. She had endless patience and never gave up on them. The Green Scapular worked wonders for all. It is no surprise to me that Sr Consilio has developed, progressed and extended her ministry to what it is to-day. She has helped and supported me on many occasions for which I will always be grateful. I am quite sure Catherine McAuley would be proud of her.

The following account was written by Liam Tiernan who was one of Sr Consilio's first voluntary workers

I came to St Vincent's Hospital, Athy in 1963, as an overseer of extension work to the hospital. I was then employed by Kildare County Council. Walking up and down outside one evening waiting for the men to finish their break, this little nun came out and asked me would I like some tea. I said "No thanks Sister." Not taking "no" for an answer, she persisted: "Do you like apple tart?" As I really like apple tart, I could not resist. I went in, and that is how I got to know her. After a while I got to know all the other nuns very well too. At that time they had no car in the convent so I used to run them here and there. Of course I had to be very careful not to go anywhere with one nun on her own - the rule was you had to bring three down in order to bring two back.

The nuns were very kind to me, especially "herself", who would always have a cup of tea and a slice of apple tart for me. Before Christmas I was moved back to Naas, and Sr Consilio was moved up to the convent kitchen. I couldn't let the festive season pass without bringing something to the nuns, so I drove down from Naas on Christmas Eve. Sr Consilio brought me into the parlour. Here was a beautiful parlour, with tall shining windows, polished mahogany everywhere and comfortable armchairs, where she had installed three of her friends. Seeing my astonishment, she explained: "I want to keep these three sober, so that they will be able to enjoy Christmas with their families." With such VIP treatment, it was not surprising that many more of her old friends from St Vincents' hospital made their way to Sr Consilio's kitchen.

The Superior - Mother Mary of the Sacred Heart - gave her the dairy - a fine substantial, unused building attached to the convent. Soon Sr Consilio realised that a lot of work would have to be done to make the dairy habitable, so she rang me, and asked if I would come down to help. Every evening for several weeks I drove down from Naas after work. In the meantime her "friends" were wandering around the grounds, and not everybody was happy about it, but Mother Sacred Heart, who was herself a woman of extraordinary vision, allowed the work to continue.

One night as I was about to go home to Naas a man drove up to the door of the old dairy and staggered in. Sr Consilio was afraid to let him go home in the car. Without hesitation, she ran across to the convent and brought over her own mattress and laid it across the stone floor. She was nervous in case he would smoke and start a fire, so I volunteered to stay with him for the night. That was in 1969 - I had been three years with her then. I continued working in Naas for a further year and drove down each night to help out.

Eventually, we were keeping more than twenty people in the dairy and it was becoming overcrowded, so we had to look for more room. We visited several places that were up for sale. In 1972 a farm of sixty nine acres came on the market - this she bought for £49,000. Later she re-sold twenty acres of this, and with a promise of credit from Buckley's Builders, plus free labour from her "friends" in the dairy, she started to build her first Cuan Mhuire in 1972. Just one year later on August 19th 1973 we moved in. We packed everything we had into a pick up truck and all the residents from that old dairy slept in Cuan Mhuire that night.

Now we had come a long way in ten years of hard work and uncertainty, then one day as we were driving along the road she asked: *"Liam, will you give up your job and help me full time?"* to which I replied "I'll think about it" - quite honestly I thought it was just a dream of hers. Working in Naas, driving down to Athy each evening to give a helping hand had become a way of life for me. However, the dream became a reality. I got ill while on a pilgrimage to Lourdes and had to be hospitalised on my return to Ireland. All the time I was in hospital Sr Consilio visited me. On my recovery I told her that I felt better and that I was going back to work. Her face fell: *"I thought you were going to give up your job Liam, and come down to help me here. Sure you might as well do it now as later on..."*

The die was cast. I rang up the County Engineer, and told him I was giving up my job. He was very kind and assured me that if things did not work out I was very welcome to come back to my job. From then on I have stayed full time in Cuan Mhuire. I became Sr Consilio's bursar. Anytime anyone gave her money, I put out my hand and took it, knowing that otherwise she would give it to the next sad case that came along. Money never had real meaning for her; whenever she saw something that she felt needed to be done she went ahead and did it, convinced that the Lord and Our Lady would provide. After more than 30 years working with Sr Consilio, I still marvel at her faith, hard work, but above all at the miracles that unfold daily before my eyes.

Sr Helen Arrives

Some years before I ever heard of Sr Consilio, at a time when the windows of the convents were being opened and the fresh air was being allowed in as suggested by Pope John XXIII we, the Sisters of Mercy over in the West of Ireland, in a lovely place called Belmullet, were having many discussions. We spent quite a lot of time having a look at ourselves as to how we could best help those in need. At that time many of our past pupils were qualified as teachers and were very well able to carry on the work we had begun, so many felt that we were now free to look at other apostolates. I was in total agreement with the idea but felt it was not for me. I thought it might be for some of the younger sisters. I was teaching at the time and loved it. I loved Belmullet and everyone in it. It is a very special place.

However, there was a certain restlessness within me which would not go away. At one of our Community meetings it was suggested that one of the Sisters would be appointed full time for visitation of the people who needed a listening ear. That was agreed and then it was suggested that the appointed sister would spend some time with Sr Consilio during the summer, to get a little insight into the problem of alcoholism, as some of the homes she visited would have the problem. I volunteered to go to Cuan Mhuire, Athy with the appointed sister as a companion.

When the time came at the end of the school year, I didn't feel like going, as I was very tired. My superior encouraged me to go, so I did. She lived to regret it.

When I came to Cuan Mhuire I was amazed at what I saw. It was really poor with very few facilities. Still everyone seemed happy and content and full of fun. I remember one character who was a very strong Kerry supporter. He used to wear one yellow sock and one green sock. He told me that when he left Cuan Mhuire and went out into "the big bad world", he decided to have a pint, but he saw Sister Consilio's face in the froth, so he had come back again. Imagine I swallowed that. I wouldn't swallow it today.

It was easy to see Sr Consilio is a very special person. She oozes welcome, warmth, love and people seem to feel secure and safe in her presence. Of course this has its drawbacks. Everyone wants a part of her time which is very draining for her. On that first visit the place was packed with people struggling with their addiction. Many had lost wives and family homes. Sr Consilio seemed to be friend, mother, and sister to all of them.

Even though the place was poor there was a great atmosphere and a great spirit among the people who were there for help. It was amazing and inspiring to see how they helped each other along. I met Sister Consilio only once for a chat during the week, but the people were marvellous and I felt really "at home" among them. It was like one big family. Of course I sat in on the group meetings Sr Consilio chaired each morning. Here people shared their problems with living, and they were gently guided by Sr Consilio, and encouraged to live from their goodness.

The first evening I was there, when dinner was announced, I was looking to see where the nuns were going. I thought there would be a special little dining room for us. After a while I noticed the few nuns who were there were scattered among the rest of the family. There was just one place left by the time I realised this, so I sat down. The man I sat beside happened to be a "Knight of the Road" and he was really funny. That woke me up. Here was a community in the true sense - all were equal - all shared the same food at the same table.

By the end of the week, I knew Cuan Mhuire was the place I was meant to be. This was my place. However I had a long road to travel before I got the permission to come permanently. I was allowed up at school holiday time, Christmas, Easter, Summer and the mid term breaks. I'm sure I was a nuisance to my superiors. At times I wished this "calling" or whatever it was, would go away.

I came eventually with the intention of helping in Cuan Mhuire. I honestly have to say that I have received more help than I could ever give. Today, we have a beautiful new building in Athy. There are three Sister Houses - one in Bruree, one in Newry and one in Galway. There is a half-way house in Dublin where some residents spend time before they venture out into a flat or to their own homes. Ask Sr Consilio how she did it, and she will reply: *"Our Lady did it."*

Our Lady Provides

I went to Cuan Mhuire, Athy in the mid 1970's, looking for help for my alcohol problem. I had been unsuccessful in many other alcoholic treatment units. Naturally, I was sad to leave my wife and children. My first impression of Cuan Mhuire was of a very warm welcome, and from there on I felt very much at home. It was like coming to a big family.

Things were not easy in those days and money was very scarce. When Sr Consilio found herself in financial difficulties (which was very often), she would always say: *"Our Lady will provide."* She has great faith in the Memorare, which is said very regularly in the house and it always works. I did not have much faith, if any, when I came to Cuan Mhuire, but it was not long before I found it. I saw it working on numerous occasions. One particular example stands out for me. Sr Consilio got a bill from the ESB with a notice that if it were not paid within seven days the electricity would be cut off. We all prayed hard that week, especially Sr Consilio herself, and to my amazement a cheque arrived on the fifth day for the exact amount in dollars. I could not believe it. I saw many other occasions in the house with other bills, such as bread, porridge, meat and groceries but again "Our Lady" provided.

Another thing that amazed me, was that the people who gave her credit or any other help seemed to have great luck. We had, and still have, 5 o'clock Mass in the small oratory every evening and our benefactors are always prayed for. The late Fr Kelly was especially faithful to praying for our benefactors.

I could only describe Cuan Mhuire as a complete miracle worked by Our Lady and Sr Consilio's prayers, her faith, and her hard work. I suppose I could say I was a miracle myself, because only for Sr Consilio and her prayers I would not be alive today. I owe my life to her.

I will never forget one night I was driving from Kerry to Bruree. About twenty miles from Bruree we ran out of petrol. It was one am in the morning. We pushed the car into a driveway for safety. It was very dark and we could hardly see anything. As time went on we got used to the dark and we saw a house about sixty yards up the passage way. We walked up and saw a Sacred Heart lamp lighting through the window. Sister prayed and prayed and of course I joined in. We rang the door bell and knocked at the windows as we walked around the house a few times, but we got no answer. We were about to go, when suddenly, again to my amazement, we saw a can on the front window sill. I smelt it and it was petrol. We went back to the car and poured the contents of the can into the petrol tank. It was just enough to take us to the yard in Cuan Mhuire, Bruree.

Some time later, as Sr Consilio was travelling that road again, she remembered that she should call to the house and explain about the petrol. Her astonished companion remarked "Do you know that the lady who lives there is now one of your nurses?". When the nurse, whose home it was, was eventually told she too was amazed as it was the only night they had forgotten to put away the petrol after mowing the lawn.

My mother was an alcoholic

I am twenty four, the eldest of seven children. I saw my mother for the last time as a full human being when she was forty one. I had just turned eighteen at that dreadful moment.

My mother was a chronic alcoholic who drank herself to a state worse than death. She was drinking for as long as I can remember. She was a secret drinker who never left her bedroom while she was drinking. She would go into town in the morning and buy her drink in an off licence - all whiskey, or when the vodka was at a bargain price, she took to that. As soon as she came home, she would rush up to the bedroom, mostly without even taking her coat off. She would spend the afternoon drinking at least the contents of two bottles, and smoking numerous cigarettes. At a certain stage, my father could not take it any longer. He took a job that kept him most of the time away from home. That left me in charge of myself - then aged sixteen, my brother of fifteen, my little sister of eight and what was worst of all, an alcoholic mother. Our grandmother - our father's mother, used to look after our clothes and give us our meals. I must say to the praise of my father that he always left enough money to cater for all our needs.

I went to the local Community School, and stayed there until I did my Leaving Certificate, which I got with good grades. I was nearing the age of eighteen. I was surprised I did so well at my exams as at the time I was under severe pressure. I missed so many days at school because, as I said before, being the eldest I had to stay at home often to mind my mother. When she would drink too much she would wander away from the house. To prevent her from doing so, I would have to sit in the bedroom with her for hours until she fell asleep. Being my mother's chief minder, I began to hate drink, seeing what it was doing to her. I even began taking the drink off my Mom and pouring it down the sink. When she would see me doing this, she would try to get the better of me, but I would not give her the drink. Then she would try anything, even physical abuse to get it. I could not understand how she could hit and thump her own daughter for something in a bottle.
Whatever happened to me, one day instead of throwing the whiskey down the sink, I got the temptation to take the bottle to my bedroom and start drinking, just for the taste of it. I wanted to

know what attracted my mother to the bottle. This happened again and again. At the beginning I would drink only a glass without even liking the taste of it. But soon I was on a half bottle of whisky neat and then I would pass out. Later I would drink a whole bottle with no after effect.

After I'd sat my Leaving Certificate there was nothing else to do but to take on the full time job of minding my mother. I turned eighteen, the magic age when you could go to the pub with friends. That was soon my only recreation. I would meet a few pals, and sometimes we would take our drinks to the park for a "kick around".

One night we were again in our favourite spot, drinking heavily under a beautiful full moon. This was a night that would never end. Or yes it did; it ended in a nightmare. Eventually, I staggered home. There before me was the ambulance, the Gardai, my grandmother, and the fire brigade. I ran upstairs and saw my mother stretched out on her bed, stone drunk and as far as I could judge though the drink-haze that blurred my vision, also stone dead. She was hauled down by the firemen and rushed to the clinic. There, the result of the tests showed that her organs had failed from excessive drinking, and she had a wet brain, useless ever after. She would never recover and was confined to her bed and to living her life as a vegetable. I was broken-hearted and while I knew I did my best for my mother on so many occasions, I was full of guilt because I was in a pub as she took her fatal spree.

At nineteen I met a lovely boy, John*. A year later we were married and eventually our daughter was born. She is now three, and she is beautiful. She has big laughing eyes and curly blonde hair. I had got a job in the local supermarket at one hundred pounds per week and John also had a good job, yet we could not manage. I couldn't keep out of the pub, I couldn't, I couldn't, I was not able to stop and I went back on the same track again and again. I hated what my mother did, yet I followed the same road.

*Name changed

Finally, John separated from me, and took our daughter with him. I couldn't care less, so long as I had my drink.

Then one day my sister came and asked me if I loved my little daughter. "Of course I do," I said, "what a silly question?" "Then if you do, you should fight to recover. If you don't do it for yourself, please stop drinking for her sake. She needs her mother... or do you really want to end up as our own mother did? Is that the way you want your daughter to remember you?" She threw the truth in my face. I felt awful, and I felt angry, but that sentence more than anything else has helped me to come to my senses.

Eventually, my family brought me to Cuan Mhuire, where I met several others the same age as myself. We are doing our best to become better people - the people God meant us to be, to live without alcohol. I have almost finished my programme; I am aware that the real struggle begins when I leave here, but I now know that it is possible one day at a time. I have been given the tools of recovery and I have been taught how to use them. I believe that, with the help of my Higher Power, my After Care, and AA meetings, contented sobriety is possible.

I dropped the heavy burden

It was a cold, wet winter's evening as I walked along Church Street in Dublin. I had been walking all day since leaving a hostel for the homeless at 9 am that morning, after a mug of tea and a slice of bread. I was totally alone. A far cry from the lovely home, wife and children that my addiction to alcohol had taken from me, along with the rest of my family, relatives, friends and a good job. As I passed the Capuchin chapel in Church Street, I heard singing from within, and for no other reason than to get some heat and company I went in. Evening Mass was just ending and I made my way to the nearest radiator. By now most of the people had left, and the chapel was quite empty. I had all my worldly goods in a plastic shopping bag, down beside me.

I became aware of movement behind me and a voice whispered in my ear: "You don't look too well my son." I turned around to meet the gaze of a friendly face. "Would you like something to eat?" he asked. He brought me through the church to a residence which I took to be the priest's house. I was given tea and toast and before I knew it I was blurting out my story. My "friend" turned out to be a priest from the church. He listened patiently as I told him about my addiction to alcohol and the horrific depths it had taken me to. By the time I had finished I was literally begging for help. He asked me if I had heard of Sr Consilio. I said I hadn't. He continued by telling me about Sr Consilio and the centre she had in Athy for people like me who had a problem with drink. He asked me if I would like to go there, and without hesitation I said I would, but I didn't know how I could get there as I had no money. I had drunk my weekly dole-money - nothing unusual for an alcoholic. He said that if I were serious about getting myself well I could call back to him the following morning and he would arrange to get me to Athy, as by then it was too late in the evening to go anywhere.

I cannot explain the relief I felt and somehow the hostel didn't seem too bad that night. I even managed to get some sleep. I had to ask myself the next morning if I had been dreaming. The next morning I arrived at the church early to meet my friend. He welcomed me and after a cup of tea and toast drove me to Bus Arus where he bought me a ticket to Athy. After getting off the bus in Athy I asked directions to Sr Consilio's place. The lady I asked the directions from told me "the place" was called Cuan Mhuire. That was the first time I heard the name that was to become so much a part of my life to this very day. On my arrival at Cuan Mhuire I was greeted by a smiling lady who introduced herself to me as Nurse Mary. She brought me into a large kitchen where I was introduced to other members of the "Family" as she described them. I was given a hot meal and some sound advice. After the meal I had a hot bath, was given a pair of clean pyjamas, some medication, and I was put into a nice clean bed. I felt human again.

I was in the detoxification unit for seven days. After the seventh day I was given different clothes as my own had become "unfit for human habitation". I now began a programme for recovery. I will always remember my very first meeting, where I heard from the facilitator, Tom*, a recovering alcoholic himself, that while I was in Cuan Mhuire I would be loved until I had learned to love myself again. At that time I had nothing left in the world except myself and Cuan Mhuire.

Today, it is a different story. Cuan Mhuire is my life. I have a good friendly relationship with my family. I try in my own small way to repay Sr. Consilio and Cuan Mhuire for all I have received by helping those wounded people who arrive for help in Cuan Mhuire. I remember Sr Consilio once saying: *"All you need to do is drop the big loads you picked up :*

(1)   Your own expectations.
(2)   Other peoples' expectations of you, as you see them.

From today on, come very gently from your goodness from moment to moment; leave all else to God and Our Lady. This way you will become your own beautiful self."

*Name changed

My Cuan Mhuire years

Despair! You don't feel despair. You cannot feel despair. Despair is something that surrounds - envelops you. It lives and breathes with you, in you. It waits for you in your bed at night and it is there in the morning when you wake. It haunts you all through the day. Like the hand at the end of your arm, it is part of you, but not you, and it travels everywhere with you. It is in the food you eat, the water you drink, the air that you breathe. It is something too awful for words, too dreadful to merit any place in your memory, and yet it is unforgettable. Such was my condition in the summer of 1992. I had reached that point which is beyond feeling, where it seemed no one could touch me and I was a "hopeless case". For it is at one and the same time truly horrifying and bewildering, to find yourself cut adrift from all that once seemed so permanent: marriage, job, status, as though it had all disappeared in the blink of an eye. So, yes, I could "see" that my life was disintegrating and that I was coming apart at the seams but, like the pilot of a doomed aircraft hurtling toward the ground at a frightening speed, the realisation of impending disaster, did not halt the downward spiral - it was "too late" and in any case, I just didn't care anymore.

I arrived at the door of Cuan Mhuire, Athy, on 19th June 1992. I had been told in advance of my arrival that I would be asked to spend eight weeks there on an intensive programme involving a combination of meetings, meditation and work therapy. Within hours of arriving there I had been introduced to many of the residents and for the first time in years, I felt a glimmer of hope - even in the midst of the blackness to which I had grown accustomed. In those days, the "old" house was the main residence and it was surrounded by a variety of prefabs and cubicles where we slept. The new building was in the final stages of completion, but I am really glad to be counted among those who knew what it was like in "tougher" times. And so in the old building we ate, sang songs and in the evening we played draughts, chess or scrabble. We laughed a lot and cried a lot and it was there that I took my first real steps on the long and painful journey of recovery.

The first job I was allocated was in the laundry. The resources at that time were very limited. The large industrial washing machine had long since given out and money being in short supply, we made do with an old enamel bath, a cold water tap, and a box of washing powder. Somehow, everything got washed and dried; and for the first time in many years, I was to feel a certain peace inside myself, in spite of all the pain which would surface at our small group meetings.

I am often asked by those who have never met her "What is Sr Consilio like?" How can I be fair to her or do her justice with a few lines in this book? "Is she this, is she that?" The best I can do is give the reader a brief account of our first "heart to heart" meeting. We had been introduced to one another briefly in my first few days at Cuan Mhuire, but it would be several weeks after the first meeting when I would break down and confide many of my troubles in her. I would come to experience the love and compassion for which this beautiful woman is justifiably renowned, and it would tell me much about Sr Consilio without her having to utter more than just a few words.

She came upon me one day in the garden behind the old house. I had been weeping silently, immersed in my pain and anxiety - she took me by the hand and looked into my eyes and as she did so, I could see the tears coming in her own eyes. It was as though she was taking my pain deep into her own heart, as though she was taking all of my burden on to her own shoulders. And those eyes seemed to see right into my very soul. In those few special moments I felt as though I were the only person in Cuan Mhuire, as if I were the most important person in Sr Consilio's world.

There are others like myself, many others, and there are those who could give their own story of personal encounters with this wonderful woman, in perhaps a more expressive manner. I write simply from the heart, as one whose life has changed utterly as a consequence of coming to know Sr Consilio, and experiencing the love and compassion which is, and will remain her enduring legacy. To love others unconditionally, to see the goodness and beauty in those who have long since given up all hope. Those friends of mine who have shared my journey will understand what I mean. When you have reached your lowest point spiritually, mentally and emotionally, and you're feeling like a worn out old boot, discarded by so many as being of no further use or value, and you come face to face with someone who sees only goodness in you, it cannot fail to move you, to touch you in a quite miraculous way - and so it was with me. I have also come to believe that the best antidote for our own lack of faith is to observe the truly faithful among us as they go about their daily lives. I have seen such faith in my mother, and Sr Consilio possesses it in abundance. One has only got to listen to her speak of her own work with addicts and others, and one hears the constant reference to Our Lady.

During my time in Cuan Mhuire I was one of those who had the great honour and privilege of making not one, but two pilgrimages to Lourdes, which is an annual event for Sr Consilio and is her way of saying "Thank You" to Our Lady for the help and support she continues to shower on Cuan Mhuire and all those associated with it. Here is a woman who does her best and leaves the rest to God and his Holy Mother - a woman who does not know the meaning of "fear", and whose boundless energy keeps her going when so many others have reached the point of exhaustion. Watch her in action as she goes to pick potatoes on the farm, or to take in the turf at the bog. She would put grown men half her age to shame! And so all of this energy, all of this infectious enthusiasm, allied to, and fortified by, the deepest of faith, has made Cuan Mhuire what it is today - a haven of peace in a world full of troubled, lonely and anxious souls, searching for peace - searching for a deeper meaning to their lives. It is this spiritual aspect of the Cuan Mhuire programme which touches those who pass through its protective and loving embrace.

The space one finds in which to meditate, and to heal the many wounds sustained on life's journey is invaluable. I have seen men and women undergo profound spiritual change in Cuan Mhuire, and so it has been for me. In Cuan Mhuire I learned to look at myself and to rediscover the good and decent man that I am. Cuan Mhuire taught me that it is futile to allow myself become a prisoner of the past or a hostage to the future and that life is now!

There are the devoted assistants to whom Sr Consilio can turn for help and support in the running of the houses. I have come to know and have great affection for many of them, people like Sr Helen, Sr

Maureen, Pat Shaw, Liam Tiernan, Noel Browne, Mary and the many caring and devoted nurses, Sr Cassie, Sadie, Marie, Terri, Carmel and many of those people have become my friends. That is the way things can develop for those who have been through Cuan Mhuire. We make long and enduring friendships and even today, almost seven years since I entered Cuan Mhuire in all my brokenness, I return regularly to Athy to see old friends and chat with them and many other family members. And now as I approach my forty third year, I am getting on with living my life - I once believed that life was destroyed beyond repair. I laugh and spend so much time with my three beautiful children. I thank God for the gift of a second chance in life and every night before I close my eyes I can see all the faces of those gone before me, and I remember in laughter as well as in tears, and I say a silent "Ave" for God's humble servant, Sr Mary Consilio.

Chapter 9

LOURDES AND ROMANIA

"And now, like Bernadette, let us live our lives as men, as women, as Christians of today in such a way that our lives have something "to tell"

"Go tell..." the Lady said to Bernadette. And Bernadette said: "My job is just to give you the message; it is up to you whether you believe it or not.".

Saint Bernadette

Lourdes

In the mid 1960's Sr Consilio made her first trip to Lourdes. Big Joe and Paddy were on their way home from a meeting in "The Dairy" - they were discussing the forthcoming army pilgrimage to Lourdes. Paddy said 'I want to take Sr Consilio on the pilgrimage' and he asked Big Joe to arrange it. Wasting no time, Joe rang Sr Consilio the following morning. She explained that she wasn't really anxious to go to Lourdes, but one way or another it would be out of the question, as Sisters of Mercy in the Diocese didn't get such a permission at that point in time. Joe was insistent that she ask the Superior, Mother Mary of the Sacred Heart, and that she do it now. Soon, Mother Mary of the Sacred Heart was on the phone explaining to Joe, that such a permission was unheard of. Joe was not to be put off lightly. He said that he understood that she could not grant the permission herself, but pleaded with her to ask somebody higher up.

Eventually, Mother Mary of the Sacred Heart condescended to ring the Mother House in Carysfort. Much to their surprise, Mother Gabriel, the then Superior General, gave an immediate positive response. Thus, the first pilgrimage became a reality.

Some events from this first trip still stand out in Sr Consilio's mind. Many of the group were going up the Pyrenees on horseback. This didn't present a problem to Sr Consilio. As a child she rode the pony to the field daily when her father returned home from the creamery. What was unexpected was that when the group descended to the foot of the mountain, her photograph on horseback was already on sale as a souvenir postcard!

Sr Consilio went to Confession in Lourdes during that first pilgrimage. The priest, to whom she was a complete stranger, spoke to her at length. He pointed out that in life much would be expected of her; that she would meet with misunderstanding and opposition to her work, but that it would succeed. He also said that she had a lot of work to do in Lourdes. She found this latter comment strange, as she visualised her trip to Lourdes as a 'once off' event. Little did she realise that two years later she would take a Cuan Mhuire group of fifty to sixty people to Lourdes, and that she would do so annually all down the years.

During her first night in Lourdes she was aware of some disturbance in the hotel. The following morning at breakfast she heard that a lady, who had gone on the pilgrimage had been drinking and the organisers were thinking of sending her home to Ireland. Sr Consilio offered to look after the lady, and did so for the remainder of the pilgrimage. For the first two days "looking after her" meant being constantly in and out of lounge bars, much to the amusement of onlookers, who saw a lady in a very short mini skirt accompanied by a nun in an ankle-length black serge habit. By the end of the week the lady was fine and Sr Consilio had gained a little more insight into addiction.

In February and March 1977 it was not unusual to see a group of men walking and jogging between Athy and Stradbally. These were recovering alcoholics preparing not only to walk to Lourdes, but to push a wheel-chair bound, multiple sclerosis sufferer. The patient was the only non-alcoholic member of the group. He had been in Lourdes six times previously, but this trip was extra special. It began in his home town, and ended fifty days later, seven hundred miles away in Lourdes. When, Sr Consilio was told of the planned seven hundred mile walk by the ten alcoholics she was very excited, but warned that it would not be easy. She passed on the advice given to her by a priest when she was thinking of opening a centre for alcoholics. *"Go ahead if you are prepared for a lot of hardship and suffering"* They were undeterred as they saw the walk as their way of saying thanks to God, Our Lady and to Sr Consilio. When Sr Consilio was asked if she feared that any of the men would drink on the journey, she replied: *"Success to me is getting up and trying; it has nothing whatsoever to do with succeeding."*

Sr Consilio recalls her first visit to Lourdes

"I remember kneeling at the Grotto and being very aware that we are all one big family in this whole world, and that we have a great Mother and Father - the Lord Himself and His Mother. Knowing this so clearly has helped me all my life. I have always felt a pull towards Lourdes and the graces our pilgrims have received through their visits could never be estimated. Our Lady is, and has been, down through the years the one who protected and guided us. She is our safe haven and our best friend.

Before my first visit to Lourdes I remember saying to Liam Tiernan who went there every year with the Oblate Pilgrimage: 'Why do you have to be running over to Lourdes when you could pray to Our Lady just as well at home ?' Having been there, and knowing all that Lourdes means to me now, I know why Liam went, and why he continues to go there every year.

For many years I went with the Oblate Fathers and worked in the hospital but as the years went on and our numbers increased I now have to devote all my time to our own group. Indeed I had many ups and downs in Lourdes and many of our pilgrims took their last drink there. On one occasion I had a run in with the Gendarmes. On another occasion we found ourselves without any hotel, but as usual Our Lady came to our aid and found us a school at the top of the town. She was actually guiding us away from hotels. Since then we have been privileged to stay every year in Cite St Pierre away from the hustle and bustle in absolute peace. Our year always begins when we return from Lourdes with a clearer vision and a lighter step - refreshed and renewed."

Romania

In April 1992 Sr Consilio was asked to speak in the National Concert Hall, Dublin. As she stepped down from the rostrum Billy McCarthy - a Kerryman, approached her. Billy was a teacher in Bolton Street College, Dublin. He was trying to organise a group of voluntary workers who would work in Romania over the summer months. He wondered if Sr Consilio would know of anybody who would be willing to help. Shortly afterwards, Billy and a friend called to Cuan Mhuire, Athy to ascertain if Sr Consilio had managed to think of anybody. Consilio had gone to a funeral so the men decided to wait. Eventually, Sr Consilio returned and when they asked her if she had thought of anybody for Romania, her prompt answer took them off their feet. *"Oh yes, I'll go myself and I have twelve others - two plumbers, two carpenters, two painters, an electrician, some nurses and a few who will gladly take care of the children."*

In due course Sr Consilio set out for Romania with her group of twelve - Mary Falvey, Mary Connolly, Paddy Connolly, Pat Shaw, Eugene McCabe, Norman Leslie, Peter Drumm, Michael Ward, Sarah Spencer, John and Nicola McClean. The group was moved to tears by the plight of the children in the Aids Hospital where they worked tirelessly, and often under difficult conditions. When it was time to return home they knew in their hearts that they had done something worthwhile with chisel, hammer and paint brush. They had in fact fitted out a laundry, renovated wards, and completed much needed electrical work. More importantly they had brought a little love into the hearts and lives of the sick, orphaned, and neglected children who were imprisoned in their cots, often unable to do anything for themselves.

Sr Consilio writes of some of their experiences

"On one of the Sundays while there, we went by train to visit what had been the King's Castle, a building of great splendour. As we travelled I was amazed to find stretches and stretches of land without a single house or human being to be seen anywhere. When I enquired as to how this came about I was informed that under the communist regime every

family in the country was ordered to vacate their homes in a matter of days and go to a flat in the city. The day they were leaving a bulldozer arrived to pull down their homes and farmyards as well as all walls and fences, so that they could never again identify where they belonged. Everything was taken over by the state and all were given equal pay regardless of how or what they worked at. This, of course, destroyed all initiative and enthusiasm. When one went into a shop nobody seemed interested in serving customers. The shops all belonged to the government. People were so poor they could afford to buy very little. Everyone seemed to be brain washed; there were so many spies about that people were afraid to speak about any situation or anything that was happening. It was easy to see the devastating effect of Communism and the trail of destruction it left behind. It was surely an attempt to blot out everything that had anything to do with the the uniqueness and the value of the human being. It deprived them of their God given gift of free will, while the state had the power to make all decisions. A deadness and lack of energy prevailed all over the place.

One wonders how blind could they be? The force of evil and power seeking was propelling them along as they tried to convince themselves and others that life could be lived independently of the author of all life. As one would expect one could sense a deep sadness and a lot of fear in the people who had no voice.

Many children - some of them eight or nine years of age couldn't speak because nobody had ever spoken to them. Some had a few words of English which they had picked up from people like ourselves, who went out to help them. They had never learned to walk or play. They knew nothing about being loved or cared about, locked in their cots from one day to the next. All of this in the name of equality, when in fact it was evil, sponsored surely by the devil himself.

Today, when I look around our own country and see all our small farms and family businesses being undermined, and done away with, as well as the whole fabric of the family which is the foundation of all society, I ask myself what is afoot? Are the evil influences eating away at the very heart and soul of our culture and our people? We are busy building little heritage centres here and there to camouflage the reality that we are losing our heritage and all that our people stood for in the past 'The Island of Saints and Scholars'. I feel we are becoming totally materialistic. Our young people are trying to fill the void that is created when they try to live at a human level - totally oblivious of their deeper, inner selves. They try to fill the void with drugs which of course leads to total disaster. Many of these young people are telling us that there has to be something more to life than they are receiving in their homes, in their schools and in their whole environment. How loud do they have to shout and how many more have to die from drug overdoses and suicide before we wake up to the reality of our situation in Ireland at present?

Wouldn't it be great if we could learn from other countries the miseries that have befallen them when God is excluded from their lives, rather than following them blindly down the same road of misery.

A pity that more of us, by our own lives, do not show our young people how to be happy and free, so that they could then give away their gifts and giftedness to each other while experiencing the great pleasure and joy that never ends."

After their visit to the King's Castle, they stopped at a park. Unlike typical Irish parks there was no fun or laughter; no children playing. However, there was a dilapidated-looking roller coaster and a man in charge of it. Sr Consilio decided to go for a ride as she felt it would cheer everybody up. There were no volunteers. Finally, Mary Falvey concluded she might as well take her chance as she felt it would be pointless coming home to Ireland without Sr Consilio, were anything to happen. Nicola McClean agreed to join them as they couldn't go for the ride with less than three people. Eventually, the roller coaster took off at a great speed. It creaked and groaned as it went straight up for thirty to forty feet and then over the top - only to descend at a more frightening speed, rattling and shaking from side to side. Sr Consilio's infectious laugh broke the tension; soon all three were in fits of laughter as they banged and knocked against each other. When the roller coaster eventually stopped, the man in charge was on his knees on the ground laughing at the trio. It was the one and only time they saw a local person laugh heartily.

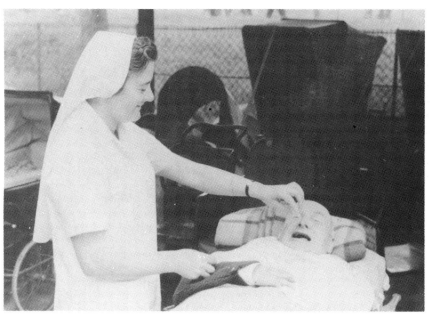

Sr Consilio working in the hospital at Lourdes

Cité Secours Saint-Pierre, Lourdes

Left to Right: **Eileen Murphy, Sr Consilio and Kathleen Maddigan in Lourdes**

Cuan Mhuire Pilgrimage to Lourdes, 1999

Sr Consilio working with children in Romania

Sr Consilio at work in Romania

Chapter 10

RECOGNITION OF HER WORK

"Let your light shine before men,
in order that they may see
your good works and give glory
to your father in heaven."

St Matthew Ch 5 V 16

Down the years the fame of Sr Consilio has spread far and near, and she has been publicly honoured on many occasions. The first such public recognition came when she was nominated Nurse of the Year in 1975 in recognition of her work and professionalism. She was away when the award was announced and when she returned home to Cuan Mhuire she found bunting and banners flying from the roof. The residents were laughing and cheering as they said "We got it, we got it," not "you got it" - confirming for Sr Consilio that they saw it as an award for all of them - her Cuan Mhuire family - not just for her.

That same year she was given a civic reception by the then Lord Mayor of Galway. In November 1977 she was nominated as one of "The People of the Year". The purpose of this award is to afford public recognition to the recipients who, through their courage and achievements, have made outstanding contributions to the welfare of the community at local or national level.

In 1993, the then Lord Mayor of Dublin, Alderman Gay Mitchell TD nominated her for the Lord Mayor's Awards, thus placing her on Dublin's civic honours list. Gay Mitchell wrote as follows: "Conferring these awards is the Lord Mayor of Dublin and the Dublin City Council's way of acknowledging the achievements of remarkable people. It is our way of recognising excellence and conferring honour on behalf of the people of Dublin. I have met many remarkable people and noted extraordinary work during my term of office as Lord Mayor of this great city. It has not been an easy task to single out the most deserving from our many worthy citizens, no matter how praiseworthy the final selection, there will always remain those who deserve to be honoured for their achievements. I feel nevertheless, that my selection will receive widespread approval and acceptance. Sr Consilio has achieved wonders with her work for those afflicted with alcoholism."

She was especially pleased when she was named Kerry Person of the Year. She was the second woman to receive this honour in the Kerry Association's eighteen year history. She was presented with a sculpture by Cliodhna Cussen at the association's annual dinner dance held in Jury's Hotel, Dublin on February 21st 1997. Marion Walsh, Cathaoirleach of the Kerry Association, said: "The award is made to people doing most for their locality or for Kerry as a whole." She also said: "Sr Consilio has vast experience in meeting suffering in others, but the serenity she radiates is proof that happiness can be found in the midst of suffering. She is a very worthy recipient of the 1996 Kerry Person of the Year Award, and Kerry people from all over the world should be proud of her humanity and achievements."

1997 also saw her named as the Athy Person of the Year. It was indeed an honour to be nominated in the town of her adoption. It was the seal of approval from the local community - their way of saying that they saw Sr Consilio's mission for the alcoholics as fulfilling an important need in Irish society. She was conferred with honorary life membership of the Royal Dublin Society. She was voted overwhelmingly as the Sun Person of the Year 1999.

There have been documentaries on both Irish and British television and radio. RTE undertook an analysis of Cuan Mhuire which was televised in the series "Would You Believe". She is well-known throughout Ireland as a result of many newspaper and magazine articles and from numerous appearances on television and radio, including the "Late Late Show", "Kenny Live" and "Hanley's People".

While she is deeply appreciative of all the above awards it would probably be fair to say that none gave her greater pleasure than the

"Hall of Fame Award 1999" sponsored by The Allied Irish Bank and The Kerryman. The Hall of Fame Award represents an impressive testament to those people who made a special and memorable contribution in their particular time. This award was special as it honoured not just Sr Consilio but the members of the Fitzgerald Family who have worked so tirelessly for Cuan Mhuire. It honoured in particular, her brother Johnny Fitzgerald, who has done so much building work in all the Cuan Mhuire centres and her sister, Sr Agnes who has worked tirelessly in Cuan Mhuire Bruree for the past seventeen years.

In the new Millennium, Sr Consilio was conferred with an Honorary Fellowship of the Faculty of Nursing and Midwifery at the Royal College of Surgeons, Ireland - an outstanding honour which she shares with, among others, Mother Teresa of Calcutta.

Apart from awards many tributes have been paid to Sr Consilio from North, South, East and West of the country. In 1985 Rita Childers, widow of late President Erskine Childers referred to her as the "Mother Teresa of Ireland" and recounted that: "During the last five years I have attended over forty seminars and meetings, most of them organised by the Pioneer Total Abstinence Association, all over Ireland. These meetings would not be complete without Sr Consilio's contribution. She never uses a script - just speaks straight from the heart, humbly pleading for those who have fallen victims of the disease of alcoholism who find solace in Cuan Mhuire. She explains in her own simple terms how she gives them love and a desire to live again. I have often noted the expression on the faces of the Cuan Mhuire residents, young and old as she speaks. They accompany her on her long drives through the night - hail, rain or snow - to attend a meeting. It is an expression of gratitude amounting to adoration of the good Samaritan who rescued them from the depths of their degradation."

(Foreword, In God's hands,
by A. Gemma Costelloe)

Des Rushe took the comparison with Mother Teresa further in his article entitled "The Power Within" (The World, October 1994): "It is apt to say that were the years of birth reversed, had Agnes Gonxha Bejazhiu been born in 1937 and Eileen Philomena Fitzgerald been born in 1910, Mother Teresa might well be called "The Sister Consilio of Calcutta". Because apart from a twenty seven year age difference, the similarity between the two nuns is total - in their work and attitudes, in their loving and giving, in their God - centredness and their involvement in human suffering, in the warm gentleness of their eyes, and the joyous serenity they radiate. In spirituality and faith they are identical twins.

Strange as it may seem there are many similarities between Sr Consilio and another Teresa - The Great Teresa of Avila. When Teresa of Avila, at thirteen years of age, lost her mother she went to the image of the Blessed Virgin and asked her to be another mother to her from then on.

Both are alike in their spirit of revolution and reform, in their sound sense and understanding of human nature, in their tolerance - advising their dependents to bear with one another; in their impetuosity to get things done; in their charm and intelligence but especially in their gift of inspiring others. Teresa of Avila says: "People have blind faith in me. I don't know why", and how many times could Sr Consilio say the very same words.

The purchase of Teresa's first convent, St Joseph's, was like the purchase of Sr Consilio's first Cuan Mhuire in Athy; they both went ahead without having any money.

Sr Consilio, like Teresa, sweeps, serves, and cooks for her family and like Teresa expects them to support themselves by the labour of their hands.

Both give much time to prayer and meditation. Teresa in her book "The Way of Perfection", says, 'Prayer is love, detachment and humility. To be humble is to trust God infinitely.' Sr Consilio's dark eyes, like Teresa's, look through the bodies into the souls of her children searching for the inner beauty that is in us all. But it is in their concept of love that they are identical. Teresa tells her nuns and Sr Consilio advises her family: "*Do not seek to be loved in return"*, which is unconditional love, the foundation stone of the Cuan Mhuire movement..."*Be tolerant, realising that background, environment and temperament form a person's personality, and accept yourself and others as you and they are.*"

They are both tolerant, not believing in petty rules and silences. Teresa was not impressed by her brother Lorenzo's proposal to get rid of the carpets in his house so as to love God with greater intensity. Sr Consilio has carpets everywhere in her Cuans. Teresa wrote: "Possessions are not important one way or another; it is attachment to them that is harmful."

The late Dr William Cade said 'I have been involved with Cuan Mhuire for fifteen years, I first met Sr Consilio at the castle which I own in Kilkea. After a short time speaking with her I was completely bowled over. At first I was a little dubious about this little lady and her talk about the Mother of God, but I was completely disarmed when I saw the thousands of people she has literally pulled out of the sewer.'

EK Barrett, Chief Superintendent, Royal Ulster Constabulary, having visited Cuan Mhuire Newry wrote: "During my visit I was struck by the family atmosphere. The effective methods used to encourage patients to gain confidence, self respect and a purpose in life again, in my view is quite remarkable. Your untiring patience, commitment and that of your staff must go a long way in ensuring the continuance of such a positive, practical approach to the problems surrounding alcohol and drug abuse. The "open door" policy is obviously working, judging by the involvement in, and support given by members of the local community... I believe you are providing a much needed service for people from all section of our society and would wish to add my support to your continuing of this work."

Very Rev W J Grant, Dean of Tuam wrote: "After several pastoral visits to Cuan Mhuire I cannot speak too highly of the endeavours of Sr Consilio and her staff. Cuan Mhuire, is of course, non sectarian and does not discriminate."

Her staunch friend, the late Cardinal Tomas O'Fiaich, then Archbishop of Armagh had the greatest admiration for Sr Consilio and the work of Cuan Mhuire, as is clear from this extract taken from his writings of January 28th 1989:

"I have been familiar with the work of Sr Consilio for alcoholics and others in need of special care for several years. I first came to know of this work during the 1960's when Sr Consilio set up the first Cuan Mhuire beside the Mercy Convent in Athy, County Kildare, during the period when I was teaching in Maynooth College in the same county. In 1977 a second Cuan Mhuire was opened in Bruree, Co Limerick. When the good Shepherd Convent near Newry in the parish of Lower Killeavy in the Archdiocese of Armagh, became vacant in 1984, I was very pleased to hear it was acquired by Sr Consilio for the first Cuan Mhuire in the North of Ireland.

Since Sr Consilio and her associates set up a community in this building, I have heard great praise for the work that is being done to aid people, especially the young, to overcome addiction to alcohol and other addictions. No one has ever been refused admission to the community and perhaps as many as four thousand persons, men and women of all ages and religions and political backgrounds, have sought rehabilitation here. They have all been treated alike, have been welcomed as persons created in the image of God to enjoy His Presence for all eternity, and they have been given fresh opportunities to live once more in freedom and human dignity. I recommend the work of Cuan Mhuire and its foundress, Sr Consilio, as work of a high ecumenical purpose, which serves people of Catholic and Protestant Churches, from North and South of the border, in an all embracing movement of Christian charity and love. I warmly commend this work."

Sr Consilio – Winner of the Kerry Person of the Year Award 1997
Many of her family were with her on the night. Front Row from left: Bernie,
Catherine and Teresa Fitzgerald. Back Row from Left: Sr Agnes, Tony, Anne,
Gerard and Joe Fitzgerald

S̲r̲ Consilio's Brother, Johnny,
Recipient of the AIB/Kerryman "Hall of Fame" Award, December 1999

Hall of Fame Award Winners, Sr Agnes and Sr Consilio, receive their presentations from John Collins, Senior Manager of AIB South Kerry; Jim Clifford, Senior Manager of AIB North Kerry and Jim Farrelly, Managing Director of the Kerryman

At the AIB/Kerryman Merit Awards, Bandon Hotel, Tralee, December 1999

Sr Consilio, winner of the Irish Sun
"Sunshine Person of the Year" award, 1999

EPILOGUE

"I shall pass through this world but once,
Any good thing therefore that I can do,
Or any kindness that I can show
To any fellow creature,
Let me do it now.
Let me not defer or neglect it,
For I shall not pass this way again."

On one of her first visits to Cork as a youngster, Eileen Fitzgerald bought a simple plaque with the above verse. Her mother hung the plaque over the kitchen fire where it was read, re-read and its message discussed on numerous occasions.

Yet, who could have foreseen how seriously the young Eileen would take its message, or how her response to its challenge would give birth to a movement which now reaches the length and breath of Ireland, and provides a service for people whose needs had long been overlooked by society.

To-day, Cuan Mhuire - the Harbour of Mary - with is four Treatment and Rehabilitation Centres in Athy, Bruree, Newry and Galway and its Transition House in Dublin's Inner City provides places for approximately five hundred persons in recovery from addiction.

The success of the movement is due under God and Our Lady to the vision and inspirational leadership of Sr Consilio; to the commitment of Cuan Muire's Directors and Trustees; to the dedication and hard work of the many people who have been attracted by the charisma of the foundress and have dedicated their lives to the philosophy and mission statement of Cuan Mhuire, which is:

To provide a context in which persons who feel rejected or dejected because of their addictions, become aware of, and learn to deal with, the underlying problems related to those addictions, and discover their uniqueness, giftedness and real purpose in life.